Advance praise for

"I am usually suspicious of 'illness memoirs' written in relation to religion, because they so often try to convince readers that since God is in charge, being sick is really okay. This book is a refreshing change from that genre. Jennifer Durant—priest, mom, wife—never tries to convince readers that having ALS was okay. Instead, she dares to say that living with ALS and dying from it, are difficult in every possible way: physically, emotionally, spiritually, relationally. And that God's love is strong and real. And that both of these seemingly opposing realities are true at the same time. This book is important for anyone seeking insight into courageous, faithful living and dying."

—The Rev. Dr. Joyce Ann Mercer, Associate Professor of Pastoral Theology, Virginia Theological Seminary

"Although the paralysis of ALS takes her last breath, it does not rob Jennifer Durant of her vibrant faith and determination to share her moving story. Read *Sparrow* and weep tears of sorrow and joy."

—Ginny Thornburgh, Disability Advocate, American Association of People with Disabilities

"There's no two ways about it—ALS is a ferocious and unrelenting foe. With unwavering honesty and luminous hope, Jennifer Durant revels how God's love is immeasurably stronger than this or any foe. I laughed, I cried, I prayed hard, and I gave thanks as I read this remarkable story of a turbulent, authentic, and ultimately grace filled priesthood."

—The Rt. Rev. Susan Goff, Bishop Suffragan, Episcopal Diocese of Virginia

"Jennifer Durant is a woman with a sparrow's faith, keenly aware of the fear of falling and wise enough to allow her spirit to soar over the monster ALS and find grace in the presence of indignity, hope in the midst of harsh reality and light as darkness slowly, surely approaches. As a Hospice Chaplain I know I will return to this book to bring comfort and solace to my patients and their families."

—The Rev. Dr. Elizabeth Kaeton, Long Neck, Delaware

"Why do bad things happen? Why do good people suffer? Jennifer Durant can't provide a complete answer to our plaintive 'Why?' but her inspiring memoir of perseverance and faith in the face of ALS shows us how to find peace by depending on the God who loves us completely and passionately—even in our most difficult and trying times."

—Anne Marie Pace, author

"One thing Jennifer Durant loved about being a priest was being able to bless God's people through the words she would offer at the close of worship. Now through her inspiring story of a holy life and a holy death her words extend an even wider blessing to all who will come to know her story."

—The Rev. Dr. Scott Stoner, Director of
Living Compass and author

"I had the privilege of working with Jennifer when she was a student and a priest. She was extraordinary then—and through this amazing spiritual memoir, she is extraordinary now. This book takes us to the heart of all the passion, vulnerability, and self-giving love any of us can hope to live as followers of Jesus, no matter what monsters in this life we must face. Thank you for this amazing last gift to us all, Jennifer."

—The Rev. Dr. David T. Gortner, Associate Dean for
Church and Community Engagement and Director, Doctor
of Ministry program, Virginia Theological Seminary

"It was Jennifer's hope that her memoir would encourage others who found themselves near the abyss of grief and loss. With poignant honesty, Jennifer speaks of the series of relentless losses that ALS inflicted. Yet, she subtitled this memoir as a journey, not a descent, for she met the unwavering presence of God, even in her dark and despairing days; and she discovered that her journey was a catalyst, which tenderly transformed all who accompanied her."

—The Rev. Tracey Kelly, Interim Associate Rector, St.
Francis Episcopal Church, Great Falls, Virginia

Sparrow

A JOURNEY OF
GRACE AND MIRACLES
WHILE BATTLING ALS

BY JENNIFER R. DURANT

WITH MATTHEW P. DURANT

 Morehouse Publishing
NEW YORK

Morehouse Publishing, 19 East 34th Street, New York, NY 10016

Morehouse Publishing is an imprint of Church Publishing Incorporated.
www.churchpublishing.org

Cover design by Laurie Klein Westhafer
Typeset by PerfecType, Nashville, TN

Library of Congress Cataloging-in-Publication Data

Names: Durant, Jennifer R., -2015.
Title: Sparrow : a journey of grace and miracles while battling ALS / by
    Jennifer R. Durant, with Matthew P. Durant.
Description: New York : Morehouse Publishing, 2016.
Identifiers: LCCN 2015030033| ISBN 9780819232472 (pbk.) | ISBN
9780819232489
    (ebook)
Subjects: LCSH: Amyotrophic lateral sclerosis—Patients—Religious
    life—Virginia. | Durant, Jennifer R., -2015. | Episcopal
    Church—Virginia—Clergy—Biography.
Classification: LCC BV4910.32 .D87 2016 | DDC 248.8/6196839—
dc23 LC
record available at http://lccn.loc.gov/2015030033

Printed in the United States of America

Contents

Acknowledgments

With thanks to . . .

My husband, Matt, and children, Chris and Kate, for your undying love and support;

Tracey and Anne Marie, for the friendship, hours of interviews, research, and compilation of raw material. Without them this book would never have happened.

Erica, the supreme writer, editor, and voice of Jennifer;

Sharon, my editor at Church Publishing for bringing my story to publication;

The Reverend David Stoddart and the entire staff and parish of Church of Our Saviour in Charlottesville, Virginia: you made my ministry possible under the most challenging of circumstances;

Acknowledgments

Bishop Susan Goff and the Episcopal Diocese of Virginia for their support and willingness to push the boundaries of the "traditional" Episcopal liturgy;

And lastly, my sermon readers: thanks for giving my sermons a human voice when I was no longer able.

Introduction

Are not two sparrows sold for a penny? Yet not one of them will fall to the ground apart from your Father.

MATTHEW 10:29

In the suffocating midnight blackness, I hear heavy breathing somewhere in the humid night closing in on my daughter and me. Certain it is a monster, a terrifying, dangerous man, I grab Kate's hand, and we dash down dark alleyways, darting left and then right, hopelessly lost. Now the breathing I hear is our own. Kate's hand trembles in mine, like the beating wings of a rescued bird.

My heart pounds like a drumbeat, pulsing in my own ears. In my peripheral vision, I see shadows gaining on us. My lungs are on fire. My legs ache and feel leaden and useless. As fast as we run, the monster's footfalls are faster. The beast grows closer. All I want is to protect my child. My baby. I gave her life, and it is my duty—the very purpose of my existence—to protect her.

We race down another littered alleyway in this unfamiliar city. And it brings us to a chain-link fence. A dead end. My daughter screams. I push her behind me and whirl around. Never underestimate a Mama Bear. I scream, "Leave us alone!" in an ear-shattering primal roar. It is my voice. *My voice.*

And then I wake up.

Tears roll down my face. And in the darkness I wait.

Voiceless.

Screamless.

The monster, the real terror, scarier than any nightmare fantasy, is ALS.

Hearing muffled moans on the monitor, my caregiver comes into my bedroom. She has been with me and my family for a long time now. She knows my looks. My "move that hair off of my face" look. My scared looks. My joyful ones. She begins the preparations to get me ready for my day as an Episcopal priest.

I have to be hoisted into my chair. I need help with toileting. I can't brush my own teeth. Despite this—or maybe even because of this—I insist on some lipstick. (My husband, Matt, has gotten pretty good at putting it on, but he draws the line at painting my nails.) I still want to look like . . . *me.* Me. So much of me has been taken by this monster, this danger threatening me, ALS. It wants *everything* from me. It wants it all, including my life. And earlier this year, in the springtime, usually the season of renewal and hope, the holy Easter season, my voice was silenced. Instead, a machine—I call her "Joy"—speaks for me now. She reminds me of the ubiquitous Siri. Those television commercials depicting this smart phone or that one, those mechanized voices are *my* voice now. But in my dreams? My dreams and nightmares are of me, able-bodied. Speaking. It is when I awaken that the reality of my body's betrayal hurtles me back. In my dreams, sometimes I fly. But when I wake up, I land with a thud back in my own body. A body that refuses to obey me, damn it. A body that the monster wants to possess.

The medical name for the disease that has stolen so much from me is amyotrophic lateral sclerosis. Some people refer to it as Lou Gehrig's disease after the Yankees hero who contracted it. Professor Stephen Hawking has a form of it and is perhaps the most famous person living with it today. Jim "Catfish" Hunter had it. So did jazzman Charles Mingus and actor David Niven. And Mao Zedong. And me. Maybe this book will make me famous too. Though I can assure you I would prefer that my fame not be for having a progressive neurodegenerative disease that affects nerve cells in my brain.

From one of my hands growing weaker at the end of my time in seminary through the onslaught of this disease taking away my freedom and dignities day by day, sometimes hour by hour, to today, my life has been utterly changed. I write this manuscript, a tiny silver dot on my forehead leaping and dancing from letter to letter on a tablet, painstakingly. Once my hands flew over the keys, a typical Type A woman living life so fully, gulping at it.

Before that, before my life as a wife, mother, and career woman—and then a seminary student and priest—I was a young ballerina. I can picture myself leaping across the wooden floors of a stage, dancing *en pointe*, perching on my toes, gliding gracefully. Effortlessly. My muscles obeyed me, and I thought nothing of it. There I was, light and floating like a butterfly, flitting in my chiffon skirt, its layers fluttering in the movements of my own legs.

Now nothing moves below my shoulders. My muscles defy my brain.

I am a prisoner in this body. I sit heavily in a chair, posed just so by someone else, like a life-sized doll. If a stray hair irritates me, if I sneeze and need a tissue, if I simply want to hold my husband's hand, someone else must move the hair, wipe my nose, take my hand.

But the monster, the monster doesn't realize what it's up against. My spirit remains *en pointe*, soaring and gliding. In my world, I am dependent on others physically, but God is my partner in the *pas de deux* of life. She lifts me high when I need to leap; he shelters me and then holds me effortlessly as I arch backward. Faith doesn't make you afraid to leap dangerously from across the stage into the waiting arms of your partner. *Faith is feeling the terror—and leaping anyway.*

So, monster, I am not done here. You will not defeat me. I am still dancing my life dance. I work at least fifty hours a week in my role as an associate priest. I bring communion to nursing homes. I counsel the faithful— and those wrestling with their faith. I teach the little ones, their faces upturned and eager, drinking in God's Word during the children's sermon. I prepare sermons and lessons—parts of which are incorporated into this book. *I am a priest.*

Those words still fill me with awe. There are many inspiring jobs out there, and many people working very hard to put a roof over the heads of their family and to put food on the table. While I receive a salary for my work, the word "job" doesn't convey the way being God's priest makes me whole. Ministry, with its three syllables, seems better suited, even weightier somehow. But my job means saving souls. When I assist someone from darkness into the light of faith, the light of us all is *that much brighter.*

I feel I have the best job in the world. I counsel those seeking a closer relationship with God—or maybe even seeking God for the first time in their lives. So, monster, my mind remains as vibrant and strong as it ever was. My work—my avocation and vocation—that part of me that cannot be suppressed, goes on. I have so much still left to do here.

When I started writing my memoir, I saw so many miracles strung together. Most of all, I saw that God knocked. I answered. When I took the "call," a term that has come to be associated with answering God's calling for a person to take up a vocation in religious work ("call" comes from the Latin for "vocation"), I was filled with such a sense of grace and peace. It was as if I was breathing God's air. I answered the call wanting God to use me as an instrument of her peace, to extend the peace, love, faith, and grace that I felt from her, out from me into the intricate web I wove. Every human weaves his or her own fabric of life. We each create the patterns and threads of our world. I could not have known that God and the sacred threads she was weaving with me would sustain me throughout this new time, the time of the monster. More than that, even, God is still using me. Every day. Maybe this is a version of spiritual symbiosis.

When I watched the Ice Bucket Challenge go viral in the summer of 2014, I was grateful to see that the warriors fighting ALS were getting attention. (I prefer to think of it that way instead of giving the monster itself attention.) I felt that the time was right to now share my memoir to bring further attention to ALS and other "orphan" diseases, those diseases that are not adequately funded in terms of research dollars. I wanted to share the utter devastation that can happen to a *family* when someone they love must fight a battle like mine. To be clear, ALS is not *my* disease—though of course there are agonies only I alone will understand—it is *our* disease. My husband's battle, my son's war, my daughter's suffering, my mother's burden, my friends' pain, my church's cause. This vile disease impacts my thread and all the pieces of fabric through which I am woven.

My church is a piece of fabric through which I am stitched, and which is stitched on my own heart. I was brought to this amazing community on my journey—a place I had no idea, when I first arrived, that I needed in quite the way that I was going to find out I did. Every day I marvel. If ever there was a community to lift up someone with ALS, it would be this one—a true glimpse of what a church family can be. A piece of heaven on this earth.

More than anything, more than this disease, more than all of the pieces of my life that comprise this memoir, my story is about faith. Everyone has a faith walk, and I am no different. I didn't suddenly earn a halo and wings by having the disease of ALS. However, my faith walk deepened in profound ways. My message to my readers is simple: God loves you. I pray you never have to walk a path like mine, but should you face dark, dark trials, God is with you. He'll meet you on the road, like the Good Samaritan, and without a word, will dress your wounds, carry you on her back, and find a place for you to rest.

My story is a story of hope and of the ways miracles and grace are hidden along the way of life. No matter our burdens, when we need a reminder of God's love, the miracle will appear if we are patient and still enough to accept it.

I named my story *Sparrow* because I am certain that like the little sparrows who fall, God knows me and knows my own very real struggle, my own free fall. Yet throughout my story of my life both before and with ALS, time and time again God has sent me signs to remind me she is with me.

I do not fall alone.

I am a sparrow. And I still soar in the clouds of God's grace.

CHAPTER ONE

Life . . . Only Better

The call of God is not just for a select few but for everyone.

Oswald Chamber[1]

Date night.

Like many married couples, date night was an important part of our lives. Our busy lives were crowded with T-ball, ballet, gymnastics, and preschool field trips; taking care of the house, and the dogs and the cat, the laundry, the dishes, dinner, school lunches; and then our careers. My color-coded calendar looked like the command post

---

1. Oswald Chambers, "Called by God" from *My Utmost for His Highest: Daily Devotional* (January 14, 2015). http://utmost.org/called-by-god/

of a general. Date night was a way to connect and take a deep breath. To remember why it is we fell in love.

My husband, Matt, and I met when I was in college at the University of Massachusetts, Amherst. I was spending the summer of 1988 working for my dad, who managed Marshfield Airport. Matt was a flight instructor—making my dad, Skip, his boss. Tricky? Yes.

I laid eyes on a very handsome, smart young man— and the butterflies I felt were mutual. It was a spark— and I am certain God *chose* Matt for me and me for him. For both of us, it was definitely a case of knowing each other was "the one." We were engaged within months, at Christmas of that same year (with my dad's blessing, no less). We were young and in love in the season of joy and colorful lights on the tree, tinsel, and the magic of Christ's birth.

Now, years later, married with two kids, we were trying—like many marrieds—to keep that magic alive with date night. We were both busy career people; we'd moved for our jobs, dedicated ourselves to the vocations we chose, him to piloting, me to corporate recruiting. Even more wonderful, a chocolate martini was being shaken. I couldn't wait to taste it. But the bartender with his jigger, the music playing in the bar area, my silk blouse and freshly done hair, none of it could wash away my nerves.

I was jittery.

I had big news to tell my beloved husband. Big news. On a par with "the stick turned blue" news. I was not pregnant. But it was a miracle all its own.

God was calling me. She had big plans for me. In fact, they were bigger plans than I even could have imagined for myself—God doesn't think in limitations. God's visions are limitless. But what I knew that night, as I sat waiting for Matt, was that she wanted me to honor her calling. I was going to become an Episcopal priest.

Yes, I was not sure how I was going to spring this on my unsuspecting husband. Matt arrived at the bar. Handsome as ever. Smiling. He had no idea what I was going to drop in his lap. I didn't think it was going to go smoothly. *God, how do I tell him?*

Becoming a priest as a mother of two, a career woman, a wife, was not like saying, "I'm joining a gym," or "I'm taking up watercolor painting or ceramics." Being a priest is a *calling*. It is not a career. Previously, I had been a headhunter, though I sold my company in the economic downturn. Still, that is a job. A calling is part of your being at its most central part of your core. And it requires the sacrifice not only of the called, but of their spouse and family too.

Now, I sat fidgeting in a bar, awaiting the perfect opening.

Matt kissed my cheek just as my chocolate martini was slid across the bar.

"Are you OK?" Matt asked.

I exhaled. Was I OK? I was more than OK. I was filled with a grace I had not known possible. I was filled with a peace that surpassed all understanding. But would Matt understand? Being a priest would mean time away from my family. It would mean, if I passed through the various hoops and requirements, entering a seminary, studying, more schooling. It would mean financial pressures. No one enters the priesthood seeking earthly riches. We had already gone through tremendous financial hardships. In the post-9/11 landscape, being a pilot became an incredibly risky career. Aside from the obvious fear of being blown out of the sky by global terrorism, airlines were merging, pilot jobs were disappearing. Matt's employer, United Airlines, had declared bankruptcy. My business had dried up. Uncertainty was all around us. And now I was going to tell Matt I wanted us to take on loans and debt in order for me to become a priest. Unlike, say, paying for law school or medical school with the hopes of one day having a very lucrative career, I wanted to minister to the sick and the lonely, the poor and the hungry, the disenfranchised and the desperate.

The adage "as poor as a church mouse" says it all.

This call of mine would mean changes. It would mean sacrifices of our family and our bank account. Being a priest is obviously far more than salary, though. A priest, like an obstetrician, comes when you need him or her.

Priests don't punch a clock. When someone is suffering and needs to be consoled, a priest can't put them "on hold" until a more convenient time.

But this call was like the clarion trumpet call, so clear, so certain. Clearly God had a plan. Of course God had a plan. God *always* has a plan. (Well, not as in a predestined plan, but God works through anything we do, to suit God's purposes.) We were living in Massachusetts, where my husband, for the first time in his life, was beginning to find true fellowship and family with the people of the congregation of the church we attended. Matt was changing. God was working in Matt, showing him that God was with us and love in community with church was possible.

But still I had the jitters. My teeth chattered, and I couldn't tell if it was what I had to tell him or the restaurant's air conditioning blasting down on me.

Matt smiled at me. "You OK?" he asked again, sliding onto the bar stool next to me.

I nodded. God, I loved his smile. *But how do I tell him?*

When you marry your best friend, sometimes they know you better than you know yourself. I decided the truth just had to be stated. Just lay my cards on the proverbial table. That simple. "I have something to tell you," I said. Then I took a *big* sip of my martini. A little liquid courage could be part of God's plan, right?

Matt looked me in my eyes. "You're going to become an Episcopal priest, aren't you?"

My mouth dropped open (after I swallowed). We had never discussed this. My calling had been deeply inner and private. It was not any *one* thing God said to me in this perpetual conversation I share with him as part of my spiritual life. It was many things.

When you are a mother, your children—when they are small—are there tugging on your sleeve at all times. You can't even go to the bathroom by yourself before you hear that familiar, "Mo-om," which all mothers of young children know is a two-syllable word. When you wake up in the morning, your children are the first thought in your mind. When you fall into bed at night, you ask for blessing upon them. In the waking hours in between, your children chatter at you nonstop. I think that I was constantly tugging on God's sleeve, always talking to her. To him. (God is too vast and wondrous to assign a gender.) And at some point, God began whispering back. Then her voice grew more insistent. But the message was always the same. Becoming a priest was my path.

However, it hadn't occurred to me that God had clued in Matt as well. Oh, how often we underestimate God. We sell her short. That is a message I deliver daily. If we only *knew* what God had in store for us, we would relax. We would exhale. We would let God do the driving, not us.

For surely I know the plans I have for you,
says the LORD, *plans for your welfare and not*
for harm, to give you a future with hope.

JEREMIAH 29:11

When Matt knew what I was going to say before I uttered a word of my anxiously prepared little speech, in which I was certain I was going to have to "talk him into" this choice, I remember the laughter escaping me, like the bubbles of champagne tickling the sides of a champagne flute.

"What do you think?" I asked.

And in typical Matt fashion, he simply offered me his support. "It makes sense," he said. "It is you, Jennifer, only . . . better."

And that is faith.

Life. Only better.

And so I embarked, with Matt's blessing, on a journey toward the priesthood. Only there were going to be challenges I could never have imagined.

Because, of course, before I was ordained, I was going to be diagnosed with ALS.

But before I even got that point, there were other challenges, not the least of which was, first, a period of discernment. In secular contexts, the word "discernment" means the ability to "judge well." Do I want to trust this person or that one? Am I meant to take this job or that one? Should I move forward with whatever plan I have for my life, or should I opt for this shiny new opportunity put in my path?

However, in the Christian realm, discernment is that plus much more. In the Christian context, I don't "judge well." I let God do the judging. I get out of the way.

Discernment is instead praying and contemplating the "call." Without getting in the way and butting in. We all need this form of discernment. I think we spend our lives, as Christians, no matter the denomination, praying to know God's will. Only we would like to give God some guidance. Remember the old television show *Let's Make a Deal*? We tell God, "I would like what is behind Curtain Number One or Curtain Number Two." We want to control the choices so they lead to what we want (or at least the runner-up choice). But I have seen over the years that God instead offers you what's behind Curtain Number Three. Or maybe in the fancy big box with the bow over there.

In terms of the priesthood, there is also the real possibility that people seriously wounded and damaged, filled with a great love for God, will choose the priesthood. Feeling it is right for them, they may not do the difficult work of healing their own pains and emotional scars so that they are truly ready to serve God's people.

After I told Matt about this call I felt, the couple we were meeting for date night strolled in. They were two of our closest friends in Massachusetts. I was beaming as I prepared to tell them the news. After all, I had Matt's support, and now I wanted to shout it from the rooftop. Like Jeremiah, I knew God had plans for me.

"I have some kind of big news to share," I told them.

"You're going to be a priest?" my friend asked with a bemused grin on her face.

Now it was *both* Matt's and my turn to be speechless. God was tugging on my sleeve now.

I had a calling. But making that become a reality meant many more twists and turns. I don't know that my path is any more twisted than the next person's. Life can sometimes bring you to your knees. And it is on your knees that you sometimes hear God more clearly. However, just because God has plans for you doesn't mean they come easily.

It's a good thing then that through Christ all things are possible.

> *I can do all things through him who*
> *strengthens me.*
>
> PHILIPPIANS 4:13

And so, to do Christ's bidding, I would move my family states away. I would go into debt. I would pare down my belongings. I would change directions so profoundly. But it was always with this quiet confidence that God had my back.

That night, we celebrated. But there was so much to come, both miracles and heartache.

CHAPTER TWO

My Garden Moment

In the depths of winter, I finally learned that
within me there lay an invincible summer.

ALBERT CAMUS[1]

One of the most haunting stories in the Bible is that of Jesus in the Garden of Gethsemane. Abandoned by his friends—even he who loved him most—and facing death, he asked God for some other way, some other path, some other life. I have walked in the Garden, at least as it existed over two thousand years after Jesus's moments of despair, on a trip to the Holy Land. As I walked the

---

1. As translated in *Lyrical and Critical Essays* (New York: Alfred A. Knopf, 1968), 169.

grounds, I could easily imagine the scent of blooming jasmine, perhaps mixed with cedar on that long-distant night. I pictured him praying amidst gnarled olive trees, their branches bent and strangely entwined, as if both strangling and struggling to give life.

I imagined the meal he just had eaten. He sat, sharing bread with his friends over the Passover supper, loving them, not wanting to leave them. But now he was in the darkness of a silent garden, utterly alone, with a grief that none of us can know—and yet a grief we all can know. Who among us hasn't had a night, a day, a moment when we felt so utterly alone that it defied words?

My own private Gethsemane was a windowless room. In a dreary, drab basement. In a world of agony that I can barely articulate. And yet even in my Garden moment, I knew God was with me—and that knowledge has allowed me to counsel people in the depths of their gardens of pain, to assure them that yes, God is with them too.

My garden moment actually began long before the day in the windowless room. It began with ALS's first symptoms. Those first symptoms were benign enough. A weak hand in my final year of seminary. I could tell something was wrong, but it was so vague—and hardly frightening. In one hand, I could grip as tightly as ever. But the other hand, my left hand, was quite pronounced in its weakness. It was also strangely clumsy. Motions

I had long taken for granted now required effort—as if directing a hand that wasn't quite mine.

Carpal tunnel syndrome. That had to be it. With the advent of Google, pop in a symptom, and you can find your answer. I also mentioned my weak hand to a congregant at the church I was attending and was told, "Go and see my hand specialist."

So I set out to find the cause of this odd little symptom. It was a nuisance, in my mind, not an alarm bell. However, as I was preparing to graduate from seminary and move toward ordination, I found myself simultaneously embarking on a medical odyssey.

There is not one definitive test for ALS. Diagnosing the disease begins as a process of elimination. I think, too, that even the white-coated people who try to remain emotionally disengaged wish fervently for something, *anything,* but ALS. And so vial after vial—after vial after vial—of my blood was taken and sent to labs all over the United States.

They hunted for the most obscure of things.

Anything but ALS.

Metal poisoning. That could be the cause. I was asked hundreds of questions over and over and over again. Some were so obscure—like out of a mystery novel. Each time I met a new physician's assistant, nurse, or doctor, I had to repeat my medical history and symptoms all over yet again, until I felt I could recite my history in my sleep. Could I have been exposed to high concentrations of nickel? Arsenic? Did my home have well water or municipal water? Perhaps the very water I drank had been poisoning me.

Anything but ALS.

What about my marriage? Was there any possibility—no matter how "crazy" it sounded—that my own husband was poisoning me? The medical profession turned over every rock, poked at every creepy-crawly underneath it, searching for something that could explain it.

Anything but ALS.

Somehow, it was as if a woman being slowly murdered by her husband, or poisoned dose by dose, day by day, was easier to accept than the disease that sends a shudder through all who hear that three-letter acronym.

Eventually, I was sent for a consultation at the University of Virginia, a respected teaching hospital near the Blue Ridge Mountains. It was there, in a windowless basement room, where I underwent an electromyography, or EMG.

An EMG measures the electrical activity in the muscles. In a healthy person, those muscles react when "shocked" by an electrical stimulus. The test, while not agonizing, is certainly not comfortable.

The person administering my test had an excellent poker face. I tried, through prayer and contemplation, to leave that windowless room, to go to my "happy place."

Because of Matt's schedule, he could not be with me that day, but I didn't have a sense of dread. I knew they were looking for serious things, but in the end, in my mind, I think it was easy to deny the worst diagnoses. These were the people, for example, who were looking for *poisoning*. Surely, this would end up being something . . . not so serious.

With each electrical stimulation, I felt a shot of pain. I breathed in and out, trying to be "one" with my breath, to disappear in that breath, to disappear into prayer. Breath. God. Amen.

After the test concluded, I was left alone in my drab surroundings. The crinkly paper on the examination table beneath me was annoying. I dressed and sat in a hard-backed metal chair, reading my Bible. Spiritually, I was in a place of such awareness of God's grace. I had spent, now, years, first in discernment, and then actually *in* seminary, immersed in God's Word.

I gazed down at my left hand as it rested on my thigh as I read the Bible. That one hand was betraying me. But the rest of me was ready for the work to be done—I had accepted a call at Church of Our Saviour, where the beautiful Rock Chapel also sits. I was ready to do God's work. Frankly, I had no time for this medical mystery.

Still, I waited in that little room.

I waited as the second hand on the oversized hospital clock ticked around, marking what ended up being hours.

What is taking so long?

Even that did not set off warning bells because I knew full well that teaching hospitals could be very chaotic places. Yet as the hours dragged on, a nagging thought pulled at me, like picking at a scab. What if it *was* something?

Finally, two doctors strode in. The news was to be delivered here, in the depressing surroundings of a linoleum-floored gray room.

With no fanfare, without asking if perhaps there was a family member who might come to be with me as we discussed their findings, without bracing me for the impact, one of them said, "We think you have ALS."

The air whooshed from my lungs as if I'd been sucker-punched.

> *Then Jesus went with them to a place called*
> *Gethsemane; and he said to his disciples, "Sit*
> *here while I go over there and pray." He took*
> *with him Peter and the two sons of Zebedee,*
> *and began to be grieved and agitated. Then*
> *he said to them, "I am deeply grieved, even to*
> *death; remain here, and stay awake with me."*
> *And going a little farther, he threw himself*
> *on the ground and prayed, "My Father, if it*
> *is possible, let this cup pass from me; yet not*
> *what I want but what you want."*
>
> MATTHEW 26:36–39

Panic filled me, and I began shaking. "What do we do now?" I grasped for straws of hope.

The taller doctor said, "There's really nothing *to* do. We'll send you to Duke for a second opinion, but we're 99 percent sure."

"And so what's the prognosis? What's next?"

Without pity, without expression, without glancing at my file and realizing I was a wife—and a mother. Without looking me in the eyes, or holding my hands. Without humanizing me. Without recognizing my soul. Without acknowledging the Bible on my lap. Without any of that, he said, "You have between three and five years." There was discussion of my immediately starting a medication to try to slow the disease's progression, but beyond that, all there was to do was fall apart. And fall apart I did.

At some point, in between breaths and sobs, I blurted out, "Chaplain . . . please . . . call . . ." If only the chaplain on call could be my friend, the same man who recommended me to the church in Charlottesville, the reason I was at UVA, and not Duke or Johns Hopkins, or anywhere else. At this horrible moment, I needed to feel God in the presence of a friend. *Please. Chaplain. Please.*

God answered the prayer. My friend walked through the door. At the sight of his face, I felt myself collapse even further, in the way we feel most emotionally vulnerable around those who know us well. On the other hand, his face portrayed confusion. He thought the call he received meant I needed him to see someone—one of my parishioners or one of those I counseled. As he absorbed the expression on my face, my swollen eyes, the tissues crumpled on my lap, the windowless room, hiccupping sobs, the testing I had undergone, shock and horror replaced confusion. *I* needed a chaplain. *I* need ministering to. *I* had ALS.

I think the next hours were as despairing as a human experience can be in this world. I crumpled. I prayed. I was prayed over and for. But I have been a follower of God for long enough to know that if God takes you *to* a crisis, he will take you through it. But that does not mean waving a magic wand and making the pain disappear. When I left that windowless room, I still had ALS. My odyssey was now more than a medical mystery. I now faced a multi-pronged medical, spiritual, and emotional crisis.

My friend and I wandered the University of Virginia campus waiting for information on the medication the doctors wanted me to begin immediately. I agonized about what I was going to say to Matt. And like any mother, my thoughts kept returning—like a compass pointing to true north, to my children. We say that at times our "lives flash before our eyes." I saw my children's births. I relived their first days of kindergarten. I saw their smiles. I wiped their tears. I saw my wedding day. Matt's and my first kiss.

And then, time spun faster and faster until I relived those words in that windowless room. *ALS*. I felt as if this was a nightmare I needed to wake from. This was not real.

I breathed in the crisp Blue Ridge air, the part of the country I had grown to love.

This *was* real. And having received the news tantamount to my death sentence, God sent a human angel, this campus chaplain and true friend who came to me at that despairing moment, when the cock had crowed, like in the hours at Gethsemane. He came to me when I wanted the cup taken from me only to know in the pit of my being that was not to be so just yet. He came to me, and in that moment, it was as if God had extended a finger.

There is that very famous painting on the ceiling of the Sistine Chapel, as God creates Adam. God's hand is extended, like a mother or father offering a finger to their toddler to hold onto as the child takes first steps. The chaplain was God reaching down, reminding me of something so incredibly powerful.

Jesus was not alone in the Garden.

God was there too.

It can be so incredibly difficult to remember we are not alone when we feel so utterly and desolately alone. But it is in those hours we must lean closer, to discern the whispers of God's encouragement.

That day brought me to a very dark place. But in the darkness is where the light of God's love seems brightest. A flashlight on a summer's day is unseen. A torch in the deep shafts of a mine collapse is more than simply light.

It is life.

CHAPTER THREE

Loved for Who I Am

> *"Real isn't how you are made,"* said the Skin
> Horse. *"It's a thing that happens to you.*
> *When a child loves you for a long, long time,*
> *not just to play with, but REALLY loves you,*
> *then you become Real."*
>
> MARGERY WILLIAMS, *THE VELVETEEN RABBIT*[1]

When I arrived at the Church of Our Saviour in
Charlottesville, Virginia, I was struck by the beautiful
triptych stained-glass window in the natural stone chapel. The church somehow looked like it had been forever

---

1. Margery Williams, *The Velveteen Rabbit: Or How Toys Became Real* (New
York: MacMillian, 1983), 4–6.

part of the landscape of the nearby majestic Blue Ridge Mountains. Trees stood tall all around it, rustling in a breeze that caressed my face and blew my wavy blonde hair across my cheeks. The Rock Chapel could be a postcard for what Currier and Ives might have painted to show an idyllic parish home in a bucolic setting. It felt like home.

Its messaging, too, was home. An "inclusive" church, a "Spirit-filled church"—the words embodied how I felt when I arrived. I was filled with Spirit. From the moment of those first whispers of God calling to me, to my actual "call" to this church, I was filled in a way I had never known possible. It was as if I was always full—swelled and enveloped with God's grace, never hungry, never thirsty, always satisfied.

For those outside the church, the way in which I came to the beautiful church in the shadow of the Blue Ridge is a bit like courting. We had talked over the phone— me and the rector, as well as members of their search committee—for hours. They had engaged in conversations with others, as well. But that *same* friend who was the chaplain at the University of Virginia had told them I would be a match. As the courting continued, it did seem as if we were "meant to be."

Despite the incredible heart-bursting euphoria and Spirit-connectedness of my call, however, there lurked that monster again. When I had first come to the church, I had a stubbornly disobedient hand. A tired arm. A confusing assortment of symptoms. But within two months of my arrival, I had received my diagnosis.

I confided to the rector—David M. Stoddart—that my unusual symptoms were actually a sign of something far more serious than I originally thought or hoped. I asked him if we should tell the congregants immediately—perhaps they would prefer a whole, *healthy* assistant rector. Or perhaps they would want to renegotiate. Maybe they would want someone who could turn cartwheels up the aisle. Not one who would soon be wobbly as she walked up the aisle to the altar. Or would eventually be wheeled up it or require ramps to roll up to the building.

I offered to do what I thought was the honorable thing: I would resign.

Rector David was remarkable. He urged that we wait to tell the congregation. His words remained with me: "I want them to love you for *you*, Jennifer. I want them to love you for your commitment to God, not love you from some sympathetic expression or outpouring because you have ALS. Let them learn to love you first."

He assured me my gifts—my God-given, Christ-blessed gifts—had not changed. That is a message for every person who feels they are less than whole. God sees us as whole and perfect. Our God talents are not lost simply because our muscles don't work like everyone else's, or because we are blind. Or deaf. Or old. Or weak or broken.

At that moment, new in that special and wondrous church, I needed to feel welcomed and "included"— because I knew, with my diagnosis, that within a short period of time, I would be more visibly ill, eventually to be confined to a wheelchair. Eventually to fall silent except for my mostly faithful "Joy." ("Mostly" because recently she deeply disappointed me by giving out for forty-eight hours when I needed her greatly—but I forgive her!) I would, I knew, be disabled. I would look different from most of the congregants. I would sound different.

So it was that I settled into life in the Church of Our Saviour. Our children found friends in the youth there. As a family, we formed bonds that will last forever— yes, even beyond this earthly place. I delivered sermons. I baptized babies. I spoke at the funeral masses for the dead. I visited the dying. I pressed the Eucharist into the onion-paper flesh of the elderly. I counseled the grieving. I counseled married couples. I met with those who had lost their faith and those who had unimaginable burdens. I met with engaged couples who wished to embark on a lifetime together. I laughed with the little children as they gathered at the altar for the children's message. I sat at picnic tables with the youth group. I fully embraced life as a priest. When I look at pictures from that time, I see a radiance emanating from me that can only be from the

Holy Spirit. From something of me and yet beyond and greater than I.

> *Likewise the Spirit helps us in our weakness;*
> *for we do not know how to pray as we ought,*
> *but that very Spirit intercedes with sighs too*
> *deep for words.*
>
> ROMANS 8:26

But eventually the monster took its toll. The relentlessness of its march was not to be slowed. Still, I was accepted—and indeed loved—by the people of the church. As a congregation, we grew together.

That acceptance, though, was not without the occasional painful encounter. When I was initially confined to my wheelchair and my voice became Joy's voice, someone approached Father David and told him I "frightened" their children and that their children should not have to experience this fear.

David's message to them was that we cannot protect our children from illness, from death, from the homeless and the poor. We cannot shield them from the imperfections of this earthly world, this fallen world with its fallen problems. This was a teaching opportunity, and if they chose to shelter their children from my wheelchair and my voicelessness, they would lose that opportunity.

Another issue came up over my role in the service. Over time, I created prompts on my digital tablet for the order of service. Seemingly countless pieces of the service—every service from ordinary times in the church calendar to Lenten times, from Christmas Eve to funeral masses. But what about celebrating the Holy Eucharist, the most precious of all my duties as a priest?

For those who are unfamiliar with Episcopal services, the Holy Eucharist is a liturgy. "Liturgy" literally means a form of public worship. But it is not me, Jennifer, ordained priest, who is doing all the work. Jesus is "in there"—at least that's how I laughingly described it to a friend of mine who does not attend any church. When I hold up the bread representing the body of Jesus Christ, he is there. When I raise the chalice representing his blood, it is more than a representation. The holy words spoken by Jesus at the Last Supper now change those ordinary items into Jesus Christ himself at the Holy Eucharist. Episcopalians believe the bread and wine become Christ's body and blood through the power of the Holy Spirit.

At some point, my hands became useless. They are generally, when I am in my power chair, placed on the armrests. Their appearance reminds me of the hands of a wax creation at Madame Tussauds. I cannot move them. Therefore, I cannot lift them to hold the sacred bread and wine, body and blood.

The question arose: Did the sacred and powerful act of Christ's presence in the ordinary bread and wine occur if I never touched the body and blood of Christ myself? What made the wine turn into Christ's blood? The bread turn into Christ's body?

And what about my voice? *I* was not speaking the words. Joy was.

Did the miracle of Christ's words uttered at the Last Supper still occur if I never touched the bread and wine?

After consulting the bishops, who are the chief priests and pastors of a diocese within the Episcopal Church (in my case the Diocese of Virginia), it was determined that yes, the words spoken were still sacred. God is greater than the mechanical act of a hand touching a piece of bread and speaking words.

God is greater than all. The intent was there. But more importantly, I was never Superwoman, changing the bread to the body and wine to blood. It was *always* the Holy Spirit. As long as my heart and soul and priestly intent were there, the act was always, all along, since the Last Supper itself, done by the Holy Spirit. In that room, as Jesus sat with those he loved for the last time, celebrating that Passover meal, the Spirit came. The Spirit filled the apostles. The Spirit transformed that meal.

The Spirit and Christ. And they are always with me. In this chair . . . or when I was a walking—cartwheeling (all right, maybe not cartwheeling)—priest.

Most importantly, I am still at that special church nestled in the cool breezes of Charlottesville. The people there learned to love me—as I am.

And is that not the walk of all Christians? To love one another as we are. Imperfect, yet perfectly created in God's image.

I am loved.

And you, readers, are too.

Love is patient; love is kind; love is not envious or boastful or arrogant or rude. It does not insist on its own way; it is not irritable or resentful; it does not rejoice in wrongdoing, but rejoices in the truth. It bears all things, believes all things, hopes all things, endures all things.

1 CORINTHIANS 13:4–7

CHAPTER FOUR

The Marriage Quilt

It takes three to make love, not two: you, your spouse, and God.

FULTON J. SHEEN[1]

When someone is diagnosed with a serious illness like cancer or a terminal illness like ALS, life becomes a series of losses. A woman with breast cancer undergoing chemotherapy may openly grieve for the loss of her hair—or her breast. Someone with lupus or rheumatoid arthritis may grieve for their health and the loss of the way they once were. They may measure their life by the

---

1. Fulton J. Sheen, *Seven Words of Jesus and Mary: Lessons on Cana and Calvary* (New York: Random House, 2001).

stairs they may no longer climb, by the things they can no longer do.

For me, with ALS, the moments of grief have been relentless, like the crashing of waves against the shore. The waves just come, cresting as whitecaps, with no ending, looking out to that horizon and beyond. Over time, I have lost my mobility, little by little. I lost my dignity in many ways—from the first time I needed help toileting, to sitting naked in a shower chair as someone else washes me. I can no longer brush my own hair or my own teeth. For a time, someone fed me—until eventually that was a loss too. I reached a point when I could no longer swallow food, so I am now fed through a tube. The flavors I once loved—chocolate and other treats—no longer grace my tongue.

But one of my moments of deepest mourning came when I was moved from the bed Matt and I chose together and have slept in since 1990, into a rigid hospital bed in my own home. I went from sleeping next to my beloved, handsome husband, the man I fell in love with that summer years ago, to lying each night in my own hospital bed, one of those contraptions that can be raised and lowered, with guardrails to protect me, as if I could roll over on my own and fall out—which, of course, I cannot.

Psychologically, I knew there would be a day when my solo bed would arrive. While I made pastoral visits to hospitalized parishioners, Matt rearranged our room, to "my" room, even removing his dresser, the twin to mine, into the first floor guest room. He tried hard to make the transition easier, with bright pink sheets and a crisply made bed. But seeing a single bed and a lone dresser where ours had been that morning was a sucker punch to my battered emotions. Everything looked rather barren—leaving space for future, necessary medical equipment. The lone bed dredged up memories of people actively dying, and I felt quite alive. How could anyone lie beside me for comfort?

I stared at the bed, and the waves of loss crashed over me, only this time, it was a riptide, grabbing me in a vicious hold. I was no longer going to be beneath our quilt, which had kept us warm through many winters, beneath which we'd made love, cried, snuggled, and invited the kids to come and read stories.

My mom thankfully suggested putting a second twin bed up against my contraption. So, next to me, I often find a black or calico cat, watching me, all nestled into my prayer shawl. Occasionally, our teenagers come sit, while Matt tucks me in. I have a mouth guard to reduce grinding. I know, so attractive, right? Despite the guards, I've chewed through the plastic. I also now have a BiPAP system[2] to give my hard-working lungs a break. As I am tucked in, the BiPAP is placed.

---

2. Bilevel positive airway pressure (BiPAP) provides noninvasive positive pressure ventilation therapy for hospital or in-home use for some sleep-disordered breathing patients who do not benefit from CPAP therapy.

From years ago I can remember the snuggle of my children. Breastfeeding a sweet babe, holding a toddler or a little one, a comfort against nightmares. Although the children sometimes still snuggle in bed beside me temporarily, we're a long way from them burrowing their faces in my neck, to hide from the world. My children have had to grow up rapidly. Our world is pretty harsh—there is no hiding from the power chair and the hospital bed. There is no hiding from the fact that I no longer speak in my own voice.

The mourning mixes with memories of stroking their cheeks, and reading Harry Potter, while they colored with crayons. "Drawing Read Aloud," we called the special peaceful time together, on the bed I don't sleep in anymore.

Some nights, Matt may come and hold my hand. When my mother visits, she often likes to sleep next to me. I know full well, you never stop being your mother's baby.

The move to the hospital bed was dictated by a couple of things. The first was simply safety. In that room, in that bed, I sleep, but I am watched over by my home nurse. She listens to a baby monitor for those sounds she has come to know that indicate I need help. The head of the bed can be raised, which at times helps with the choking feelings associated with ALS. Because my feet swell with water retention, instead of raising them above my heart with pillows, the contraption makes them higher with the push of a button. And to save my helpers' backs, the entire bed goes up and down. Who would have thought a bed could be so exciting?

The second reason was Matt's health and well-being. As a pilot, he needed sleep—it's an actual requirement of pilots that they get adequate rest. As the toll of ALS dragged from months past the year mark and beyond, the toll on him was evident. Eventually, through a generous aspect of the pilot union's contract negotiations, he was able to take a sabbatical/leave to care for me. Still, sleeping next to me, the fact was, Matt never slept. He likened it to parenting a newborn—in particular that first newborn.

When you bring your first baby home from the hospital, pink and rosy and smelling like newborn heaven, for the first days and weeks you never sleep through the night. Beyond waking for the two o'clock in the morning feeding, it's listening. The endless listening in the darkness, in the stillness of your house. You listen for the rise and fall of the baby's breath. Is the baby still breathing? (By baby number two or three you learn to relax a little.)

For Matt, hearing me struggle in my sleep, the gurgles caused by difficulty swallowing, the restless breathy sleep of ALS, kept him awake. Without sleep, Matt's own health—both physical and mental—deteriorated. The move to that hospital bed was needed.

But it didn't make it any easier, any less painful, any less than an act of mourning and grief. ALS has stolen so much—even my marital bed.

Yes, I mourned our bed. Leaving it was so incredibly painful. For the bed was far more than the queen-size mattress beneath the comforter in our cozy room. Sharing the bed symbolized our unity. It represented the promises we made long ago at an altar.

In sickness and in health.

Marriage preparation in the Episcopal Church is left to the discretion of the priest who will perform the state's legal requirements. The service follows the Book of Common Prayer's Celebration and Blessing of a Marriage. Holy Matrimony. Those two words that are in the first sentence of the opening prayer following "Dearly Beloved" tell you that marriage in the church is different from marriage at city hall. The rings, those gold or platinum symbols of fidelity and commitment, are an outward sign of the union between man and woman. But in Holy Matrimony, God is a participant. God is there. Just as Jesus is present at the sharing the Eucharist.

> *I therefore, the prisoner in the Lord, beg you*
> *to lead a life worthy of the calling to which*
> *you have been called, with all humility*
> *and gentleness, with patience, bearing with*
> *one another in love, making every effort to*
> *maintain the unity of the Spirit in the bond*
> *of peace.*
>
> EPHESIANS 4:1–3

At the Church of Our Saviour, we guide couples through six preparatory sessions in which we introduce them to the spiritual idea of Holy Matrimony. We examine both the sacred—such as the vows and the beautiful words the Bible has to say on the subject—and the profane. We cover items mundane, such as whether the couple has discussed their feelings on dividing household chores. (I can tell you after years of studying for the priesthood as well as being a priest that as in love as a couple may be when they arrive for the six sessions, many of them will one day scream at each other over items as ridiculous as leaving dirty socks on the floor or someone not changing the toilet paper roll—and sorry, gentlemen, you are usually the guilty party there . . . I hate to say it, but there is no Toilet Paper Fairy.)

We also cover the sacred. How will you invite God into your union, how will you raise your children within a faith? We urge couples to pray together.

However, beyond my priestly duties related to marrying engaged couples, marriage has a personal meaning for me as a wife. And as a mother. You see, with ALS, mothering becomes urgent. I want to fill my children's hearts and minds with all the wisdom, love, and ideas I long for them to absorb from *me*. Not from a book, or from a talk show, or even a neighbor or friend. *I* want to be the one to talk to them about finding a life partner.

I want my own marriage to illustrate the ideals I hold dear. I hope when my children find their own mate they will embody these wishes and hopes and prayers.

These are the beautiful whispers for my children—and for my readers. Your shared bed should be a sacred place. Hold it dear. Here are my bits of wisdom for marriage:

- The best relationships are founded on friendship. Yes, Matt was handsome. Yes, my blonde hair blew like a supermodel's (work with me here). But the very origins of our marriage and our relationship is a friendship. In other words, "loving-kindness." Realize the warm fuzzies are probably going to wear off. Rarely is a lifelong union about romance. A decade into your marriage, you are not likely going to sit on the couch like the early days and "make out." Chances are the little game you played of "You hang up first," "No you," during your late-night calls are going to give way to, "Can you stop on your way home from work and get Pepto because I've got food poisoning?" or "Darn it, will you please put the seat down, so I don't fall in at two o'clock in the morning?"

- Wait at least two years before having kids so you can be a couple before you're Mom and Dad. I know women, in particular, can find themselves with an empty nest, having fully worn the "Mom" superhero cape for so long that the couple identity is a misty memory.

- "Marriage is hard work" is an understatement. It's easy to fall in love. Marriage is the hard work. And most people will tell young people, "Marriage is hard." But we lack specifics. Maybe we're so delighted to be around new love, that joy (who doesn't love a wedding?) that we don't want to dampen the excitement. But we need to teach young people just how difficult marriage can be— this is so important, so utterly important. We don't tell them about the nights when you're changing sheets three times because the kids all contracted a stomach bug at the same time. We don't tell them that you won't look sexy and desirable with those circles under your eyes and twenty extra pounds. We don't tell them about toxic in-laws, and the sexy neighbor next door with designs on your spouse. We don't tell them about the lean months with more bills than money in the checking account. We especially don't tell them that is the month the water heater will blow.
- There's no happily ever after. Not the fairy tale way. There will be horrible times, but also amazing blessings. The happily ever after is looking over, and seeing the love in your spouse's eyes when the doctor has bad news, or your teenager confesses to drug use, or your own parent dies and you are awash in waves of anguish.

- Make a healthy church your center. Jesus was always in community, and that's where it's easier to see God at work. Healthy churches aren't always easy to find. So choose your church wisely—and then commit to being part of its fabric and roots.
- Make the choice to be married to your partner every day. Don't walk away when the road twists and turns.
- Communication. A simple word. So difficult to actually do well. Communication isn't just talking either. It's listening with an empathetic ear.
- Appreciate each other. Find one thing to love about your spouse each day. Find one thing special. Some days, it might be so difficult that the thing you love could be "she's sleeping" or "he's hiding in the garage working on the car." But other days the appreciation items might fill your heart to bursting.
- Get help when you need it. See a counselor, or me! Visit your priest or minister. Or find a couple whose long marriage you admire and use them as mentors.

I miss sleeping next to my husband. I miss holding Matt's hand. I miss our lovemaking. I miss hearing his breathing in the comforting way it can be to sleep next to your spouse at night. But I know my marital bed is more than that queen-size bed. It is the sum total of our years, our children, our lives. It is Christ and God there with us, uniting us in love.

And love . . . love is far, far stronger than ALS. It is the quilt that will keep us warm, together.

CHAPTER FIVE

Footsteps

*As you walk through the valley of the
unknown, you will find the footprints of Jesus
both in front of you and beside you.*

CHARLES STANLEY[1]

Most Christians are familiar with the story that has
come to be known as "Footprints." In it, a man's spirit
goes to heaven and reviews his life on earth, which he
sees as a path along the beach in the sand. Sometimes,
two sets of footprints appear, side by side. Other times,
only one set appears. When the man asks God about it,

---

1. Charles F. Stanley, *A Touch of His Freedom: Meditations on Freedom in
Christ* (Grand Rapids: Zondervan, 1991), 45.

he says, "But Lord, you promised to always be beside me. Why can I only see one set of footprints at the darkest times of my journey?"

God gently responds, "My child, when you see only one set of footprints, it was at those times that I carried you."

Who among us hasn't been carried by God at our weakest moments? This story has been put on everything from refrigerator magnets to coffee mugs to Christmas ornaments to prayer cards. I know it resonates with people—as it does with me. Now that I cannot walk, I like to think that God is carrying me.

Footprints. Never did the concept have so much meaning to me, though, as when I traveled to the Holy Land.

In 2010, before I noticed the troubling symptoms of ALS, I was blessed to go on an eighteen-day journey to the places I had long read about in the Bible and imagined. I would be walking in the dusty paths of Jesus himself. I would be walking in the shadows of his footprints.

The trip was a once-in-a-lifetime experience. The memories are a part of my being. We can sometimes forget Jesus was both God . . . and man. The stories of his miracles and his life as a son, friend, healer, prophet, and person are so holy to us that it is easy to picture him with a perpetual halo, as depicted by the great painters of the Renaissance, glowing in some magical fashion. We forget he was a man. That his dusty sandals walked along the

Sea of Galilee. That he broke bread with his friends. That he slept in simple stone homes. That he was his earthly father's apprentice, a carpenter. He had callused hands.

When I picture him—particularly after my trip, which humanized him even more, while making him even more godly in my heart and soul—I imagine dark hair, dark skin. He wears a tunic. He is barefoot. He has brown eyes, and they don't just see me, but they see *into* me and through me. They see me as I truly am—warts and all.

That is how God sees us all. This is why lying to ourselves—and God—is an exercise in futility. God knows us, deeply and truly, in a way even those of us happily married for many years cannot know our own spouse.

In the Holy Land, I walked among the real sites and places Jesus walked. One of the most famous stories in the Bible is of Jesus clearing the money changers' tables. As a story, what sticks with me is that we see Jesus's anger on behalf of his father.

I feel righteous anger sometimes. Not at the inconveniences of life—the traffic jam, the misplaced keys, the rude person in front of me on line at the grocery store. No, I feel anger akin to Jesus's at the new statistic that 51 percent of the children in the United States live below the poverty line. I feel anger, like Jesus's, when I see children's bodies in bags in war-torn countries. I feel it when I imagine women being raped as an act of war in countries around the globe. I feel it when I hear hate-speak being uttered about minorities or those people label as "less than" or "other."

On my trip to the Holy Land, I got to visit the Temple Mount in Jerusalem. This placed me on the same hallowed ground (though several feet above, technically) where Jesus cleared the temple of money changers. In the fifth century, the Al-Haram ash-Sharif Mosque, also known as the Dome of the Rock, was built to provide an Islamic focus in the Holy City. As Christians, we could not go inside, but I was able to take photographs. I find it quite amazing that all the beauty and intense love shown to God in this place is wrought with strife and filled with crowded tourism. Traveling with other pilgrims, we were actually—aside from security—very much left alone, despite all the crowds.

I was breathing the same air as Jesus. I could place myself in his footsteps, imagining him coming into his father's temple. I could understand his being so upset at the sight of those disrespecting what the temple should have been.

It saddens me to think of the Holy Land, divided and violent at times. Oh, but that we could all walk in the steps of the Prince of Peace.

The holiness of Jerusalem is overwhelming in so many ways. In this holy city, Jews, Muslims, and Christians exist openly together—times of coexistence in between bursts of violence. This is a holy city where muezzins call five times daily to everyone in hearing proximity to the mosque for Muslim prayers. This is a holy city that builds church after church, bigger and bigger, mosque after mosque, bigger and bigger, to honor our God. Yet it is a holy city that cannot live peacefully.

I worshipped so completely in Jerusalem. I turned to God at the call of the Muslim prayers, for Islam is an Abrahamic religion. I turned to God in my own morning silence. I turned to God at the Holy Sepulchre, and I turned to God by placing my ear on the altar with the Greek Orthodox priest at their church.

God's bigness, his universality, is everywhere in the Holy Land. Jesus's sandy footprints were my path there. And remain my path still.

In the Holy Land, we walked down the hill to the Garden of Gethsemane, that place I referenced earlier, olive trees growing and twisting, ancient and gnarled and scenting the air. The beauty of the church at the garden is inside as well as outside. The incredible stained glass purple windows reflect Jesus's Passion. Inside, there stands a rock surrounded by a crown of thorns.

As my own suffering has intensified in the years since my visit, I meditate on that crown of thorns. My savior suffered, and in that deep and profound suffering he understands my suffering.

He understands your suffering.

There is a place at the Church of the Holy Sepulchre where you can touch the rock ledge, the location of

Christ's crucifixion according to Queen Helena, who found three crosses in what is now the basement of the church. As I came back down the stairs from the ledge, I encountered a Greek Orthodox priest. I came to learn his name is Saleem, and we made eye contact. That alone is a bit nerve-wracking in this foreign land.

I thought, "OK, I've already blown it," and I offered him a tiny smile. He smiled back, and we fell into step together. Something in me led me to look over at him and say, "Isn't it wonderful that we're all here together?"

He responded, "Paradise." Then he said it again. Then he told me he had been a priest in the church for seven years but had been coming to the Holy Sepulchre for over twelve years. He asked my name and then said he'd give me a tour of their most holy places. He took me around, a truly holy and blessed experience.

He shared his faith with me through the things in the Holy Sepulchre that meant the most to him. We went into Christ's tomb, and he showed me a big crack in the wall. He told me the crack has been there for two thousand years, still having the smell of those two thousand years. He inhaled, smelled the crack, and I followed suit. I smelled the incense for sure, but I tried to absorb it all as "the smell of two thousand years ago"—the smell of Jesus's time. Then we touched the stone covering over what was Christ's tomb, which also has a crack, on purpose, to keep the Crusaders from stealing it, which they were prone to doing. We also sniffed that crack, and there were candles in there up higher, and I learned how the fire lighting them is the same fire from two thousand years ago. Think on the incredible holiness of the act of keeping the flame alive.

These moments weren't like my time in seminary, they weren't about the book learning, research, and studying I had undertaken. This was experiential. Then my new friend took my hand in his, and we lifted both our hands up to heaven. He prayed something in his language including my name. When we turned to go out, I faced away from him and as I took my first step out, he put his hands on my upper arms, and issued what in hindsight I believe was a blessing. He included my name and something like, "You will be fine, you will be blessed . . ." But it all happened so fast. Standing in front of Christ's tomb, the power and energy were extraordinary. I felt as if Jesus himself had led me here—I had followed his footsteps to this moment.

We then hurried out to the front where my newfound guide showed me another crack in a column made two thousand years ago. Again we smelled the scents of Jesus's time. My friends from the trip were outside and saw us, and looked at me as I followed the priest back inside to a stone altar. He put his ear flat on the altar to listen for the sounds of the soldiers hitting Jesus on the head. He gave me the idea that I might not be able to hear, since it was my first time, but I tried anyway. This altar is over a stone stool where the priest said (and the painting above shows) Jesus sat with a crown of thorns and received whack after whack. After this, I thanked him, and the two of us wandered back out to the courtyard where my friends were sitting. I introduced him, and we then headed back to St. George's College, our home away from home. Where was God in all this? You tell me. I believe he was present in the whispers that reached across two thousand years.

On our trip, we also visited the Church of the Visitation, where Mary went to visit Elizabeth as told in Luke 1:39–45. At her visit, the child in Elizabeth's womb, John the Baptist, leaped upon realizing Jesus was in Mary's belly. This site was pleasant and low key, a beautiful church that sits high above Jerusalem closer to Bethlehem. We then walked down the street to where John the Baptist was born.

John the Baptist. The man who blessed Christ in the river. Another real man. Not just a storybook character.

The highlight of the day was supposed to be the Church of the Nativity, the presumed spot where Jesus was born. It is marked with a Hollywood style, fourteen-point star, to note the fourteen generations. Somehow, this seemed so commercialized, so far removed from the humble babe in a manger, born of a teenage, frightened mother, on the run—on a slow-moving donkey, no less—from an evil king who would slaughter all firstborn sons. Yet I knew the air I breathed was somehow part of my faith.

In the midst of my trip, I bathed in the Dead Sea. You can only float for maybe fifteen minutes—the Dead Sea is literal. Nothing can live in its saltiness. But I floated, there beneath the burning Middle East sun.

The trip was the trip of a lifetime. It was a trip that filled me so fully with faith. It spoke not just to my soul, but also to my senses. I felt the sun on my face, the salt against my skin. I smelled the scents of two thousand years ago. I heard the call to prayer five times a day from the mosques. I heard whispered prayers in sacred churches. I tasted persimmons and the fruits present during Jesus's time. I touched my fingers along the rough stone of the Wailing Wall.

I walked along the dusty roads my savior walked.

And now that I cannot walk, those memories are all the more precious.

But now that I cannot walk, I know more fully, it is when we cannot walk that Jesus carries us.

I had no way of knowing then what I know now. That in this moment, there is only one set of footprints in the sand. I am being carried. But then again, when I think of the sights and sounds and senses awaked on my trip to the Holy Land, I was being carried all along. God was leading me.

And I followed.

CHAPTER SIX

The Care and Feeding
of a Priest—and Her Flock

Too often we underestimate the power of a
touch, a smile, a kind word, a listening ear,
an honest compliment, or the smallest act of
caring, all of which have the potential to turn
a life around.

LEO BUSCAGLIA[1]

Let the little children come unto me and forbid them not.
In the simple yet heartfelt command of Christ from the
Gospel according to Matthew (19:14), we have such an

---

1. Leo Buscaglia, *Love: What Life is All About* . . . (New York: Ballantine
Books, 1972).

image of Jesus. It is an image of him those of us who love Christ hold dear.

Children, you see, love Jesus in a way we all would be wise to love him. If you are ever feeling particularly cynical about the world, if you're ever feeling the tendency to doubt faith, and to wonder if God even hears your prayers anyway, I advise you to go to church and observe the children during a children's sermon.

They squirm. Kids do. Oh, yes, their parents and grandparents are probably whispering under their collective breaths, "Sit still and listen," but kids squirm anyway.

Kids will also ask the most embarrassing questions— or give answers to the priest's questions that will make Mom and Dad blush. "Did Jesus wear underwear?" "Is Jesus friends with Santa Claus?" Kids will burp loudly during the quietest moments, or they will pinch their kid sister and make her cry during the blessing.

But aside from that, when the priest asks them a very simple question, "Do you love Jesus?" the answer will be a resounding, "Yes!" with an enthusiasm that will rattle the rafters. Ask a group of preschoolers and kindergarteners to sing "This Little Light of Mine," and I promise you, your eardrums may vibrate a bit. They sing their love of the Lord loudly. They proclaim their love in the most passionate and honest manner possible.

We can learn a lot from them, actually. These little children are the innocent lambs following their Shepherd without question.

So it is that I love the image of Christ as Shepherd. Sometimes, it is the simple lessons of children and the Lord that are the ones we must take closest to our hearts.

When I came to the Church of Our Saviour, I was fortunate enough to arrive at a vibrant, living, Christ-centered church, a church that serves as a shining example of what a church can be. We're not perfect. In fact, thinking your church is unassailable and perfect can be the first step in a downward slide. But we have with great love and dignity served each other.

When I arrived, it was I who tended my "flock." A priest's work is never done. But oh, how I thrived on the work to be done. There were babies to baptize and the sick to visit. I had sermons to prepare and Bible studies to lead. There are also "business" aspects to being a priest, and we had large projects to attend to—a new building whose foundation needed to be poured, for example. All the work I did was part of the care and feeding of my flock. Like the shepherd image we often see in artwork of Jesus as shepherd, I imagined myself literally holding lambs—the people and families I grew to love.

And then I was diagnosed with ALS.

At first, the changes were subtle. A weak hand. An unsteady gait. Then, little by little—and then a lot by a lot—the disease wrought horrific developments. Eventually, I suffered a terrible fall on the sidewalk outside church and was injured. After that, I realized that I wasn't Wonder Woman. (All right, I secretly still have my blue cape . . . but. . . .)

After that fall, my weaknesses were even more exposed.

How many of us hide our weaknesses? What is your hidden weakness? For some, it might be a disease—a hidden disease others can't see. One person might have MS. Another might be diabetic. It might be alcoholism or drug addiction.

Weaknesses might be those secrets we think we're hiding—even from God. But I have news for you. God sees you berating your stepchild but favoring your own. She sees the ugly e-mail message you sent in a rage but thought better of once you calmed down—she was looking over your shoulder when you were writing it, probably urging you through your conscience to consider its contents. But that finger of yours still pressed "send." Nothing is hidden from God. Not the way you treat your family—or the way you treat the homeless.

God also sees the shame you carry. Maybe your soul sicknesses have caused you to do things you do and should regret. But God also sees the shame you carry that you should put down right now. How many of us *still* hear our father or mother telling us we are unworthy, or childhood messages that have no business following us into adulthood?

God sees your depression, your grief, the days that getting out of bed requires Herculean effort. God sees it all. Just as God saw my fall outside of church.

For me, every sacrifice I made because of ALS was one I made kicking and screaming—even after I could not kick and scream anymore. I didn't want the power chair. I certainly didn't want my handicapped van.

In fact, the van was even a source of marital tension. My beloved Matt is . . . well . . . a *guy*. And though it is a generalization, many men, when faced with a crisis in their family, want to *fix* things. The whole men are from Mars and women are from Venus thing has some points. Men are the ones with the Craftsman tools in the garage. A pipe bursts, and they go get a wrench (or call the plumber). The car has a flat tire, and they change it (or call AAA).

Matt cannot fix ALS. So he did the next-best thing. As my condition deteriorated, he went and bought a handicap-accessible van. He did it without consulting me. I've tried to think of a relatable analogy for this, and the best I can come up with is if, ladies, you casually mentioned you wanted to spruce up your wardrobe, and you came home from a long day at work one day to discover your entire closet had been cleaned out, down to you last pair of panties—and replaced with clothes not of your own choosing.

The loving intent was there, but I felt blindsided. With the wisdom of hindsight, I realize I still had not fully reconciled myself to being completely dependent on others.

But that time was coming. That time arrived.

As time went on, as the disease progressed, I kept tending to my flock. But more and more, my beautiful and loving flock tended to me.

Here are but a few of the ways this wonderful community of the faithful has taken care of me and my family:

The first thing I think of is the choir director putting my hair in a ponytail so I could go to the gym. And at the gym, parishioners in my same class helped me get my bench step in place, when my hands were getting weak.

About that time, it became challenging to hold the paten, which is the special plate the consecrated bread (hosts) is placed on. The Altar Guild went out and bought a paten I could hold more easily (for a while).

When we moved, out of necessity, from our two-story colonial to our ranch, more than fifty (!) people showed up to move us, including the youth minister's husband who moved us with a box truck he borrowed from work, and a couple who paid for movers to move the big items. Another couple provided lunch for all on the front lawn. They moved us in right down to a cleaned, unpacked kitchen and a china closet. I think we might have had one or two unpacked boxes. The shed was even organized. One couple coordinated the whole move itself, and I think I only devised a color-coded system. The boxes going from the kitchen to the kitchen were green, dining room blue, and so on. No one in the history of the special "heck" that is moving has ever has such a smooth and wonderful relocation.

When my walking grew shaky, I always had someone on my arm to steady me. You know that song "Lean On Me"? I leaned. They made sure they were there to lean on.

When I could no longer drive myself (my arms grew too weak to move the steering wheel), they drove me to and from work, and on pastoral visits. At first, they just helped me in and out of the car. But eventually, I needed something else, and a parishioner had a scooter in her basement. It was portable, and Matt trained about thirty people on how to put it together and take it apart.

They drove my daughter's carpool, with me riding shotgun. And think about that loving gesture in and of itself. It would have been far easier to exclude me from that ride and just pick up Kate and take her. But they didn't shut me out of my own existence. They took Chris for last-minute school supplies. Every parent knows that "Mo-om! I have a project due and I need three blue pencils and three red pencils, a 22-by-28-inch piece of poster board, and glitter glue. . . . Oh, and Mom? It's due tomorrow."

They have been providing meals every Thursday for over two years now, and someone inevitably drops off another. My family eats very well.

Speaking of care and feeding . . . I am fed. Literally. At church potlucks, someone would take a turn feeding me, with a fork for me and a fork for whoever was doing the feeding.

They remodeled the altar area, called the sanctuary, which was planned before I arrived. But the actual work never took place until I was wheelchair-bound. They added ramps for accessibility.

Now, I have a group who reads my sermons, with Joy doing the final few sentences.

They turn my arm and hand so an acolyte can place the hosts into it, and parishioners receive from me. And though I mentioned earlier that the ordinary was still turned into the extraordinary through my blessing, the fact is having that host in my actual hand was important to me. It kept me connected to the people I loved so dearly and the church that is so much a part of my heart.

They've supported my family and me and the ALS Association's annual walk, and the Ice Bucket Challenge, in person and with monetary gifts and gift cards to help however they can.

Jesus and his lambs. I love the imagery. And now the lambs somehow protect the shepherd.

I know every church is not a healthy church. Sometimes, a priest's hardest work is undoing the pain of people who have been hurt by churches.

That seems such a strange statement. An oxymoron. Churches, the very intention of churches, are to be places where "two or more gather" in Jesus's name. In fact, the role of the Church is so important to Christians that the Church is referred to as the "bride of Christ." If you soak in that statement, imagine the traditional vision we all have the beautiful bride. She is there, pure and beautiful, in a lovely gown, and for most women, they will never be more radiant than on their wedding day. But when the bride of Christ is treated as a bride, is cared for and loved and raised on a pedestal, *I am here to tell you that miracles can happen.*

> *Husbands, love your wives, just as Christ loved the church and gave himself up for her.*
> EPHESIANS 5:25

Unfortunately, it does not always work that way. People are sometimes damaged by—not Jesus or God—but the failings of God's people. We have all heard stories of churches torn apart by infighting, finger-pointing, schisms, and the like. Suddenly, people who worshipped together for years, through potluck suppers and prayer meetings, Bible studies and baptisms, can hurl invectives at each other as if they were mortal enemies. Sometimes it's over "important" issues—perhaps a priest or elder who has had an affair or damaged the church in some way. But more often than not, it can be something as seemingly insignificant as altar cloths or hymn choice.

But when a church holds dear what it means to be a church family, when a church realizes that together, with God present, it is stronger as a sum of all its individual parts, that's when you just stand back and marvel at the blessings.

Jesus is our Shepherd. We are his flock. When we trust him the way the little ones at children's sermon trust, you walk (or wheel) into the building and sense something special.

I am the miracle of the Church of Our Saviour. I may not be able to walk. Or talk.

But my flock?

They have my back.

CHAPTER SEVEN

The Broken Wing

The wound is the place where Light enters you.

RUMI

It is the thief in the night.

This thief is ALS. I can't fully list all of the things it has stolen from me. First, of course, it took my body, piece by piece, muscle by muscle, nerve by nerve.

It took my mobility. I went from feeling a little unsteady, to needing a cane and support, to being in the power chair sometimes . . . to being in the power chair full time.

ALS stole my voice. From a tremor in my speaking voice to a chronic hoarseness, to my voice slipping away, seemingly a breath at a time, until now my only speech is mechanized.

ALS took intimacy from me. Privacy. All of the most intimate parts of my life, from toileting to bathing, to being fed (until I was switched over to full nutrition in a feeding tube)—are handled by others. I had to become used to aides being around me—whether I was naked, dressed, looking put together, or messy and unkempt.

It fundamentally changed my marriage. My marriage, at times, is a triangle—me, Matt . . . and my caregivers and overnight helpers. I went from feeling an equal to my husband to being dependent on him for everything, right down to brushing my teeth.

ALS changed how I parent. Seemingly overnight I went from being the typical suburban "command central mom"—the person who kept track of all the activities and soccer games and school projects—to being on the sidelines. Matt makes most of the command central decisions now. And even when the kids try to include me in the decision-making, I know it's that they're making the effort, not that they *need* me in the middle of the process. After all, I can't drive them anywhere. And the mother-daughter moments I have looked forward to since my daughter's early life—when one day we would go for those manicure-pedicure outings and shopping trips, the switch from "mommy and me" moments to the beginnings of a real friendship—have been stolen too.

I feel like Sisyphus pushing the rock up the mountain. No sooner did ALS rob me of something than I found a "work-around." Initially, the work-arounds were smaller—a specially designed paten, or a belt to secure me in a chair. But over time, work-arounds were no more and, instead, major changes to my life were necessitated.

Yes, know that I hate the thief in the night that is ALS. And as much as I hate ALS, as much as I know that ALS will keep gunning for me, like I have a bull's eye on me, I am not 100 percent certain I would choose to never have had it.

I have to clarify and be precise here for a moment. If I could wave a magic wand and make ALS disappear for the 5,600 Americans who will be diagnosed with it this year, the tens of thousands with it around the U.S. and around the globe, I would. Right now. Abracadabra.

But would I choose to take it away from me?

Only me? I don't think so.

The Lord is near to the brokenhearted
and saves the crushed in spirit.

PSALM 34:18

God gives us many gifts. Sometimes we don't recognize them. We are gifted with a beautiful sunrise, but we sleep through it. We are gifted with a beautiful day on the beach—but we're so busy keeping up with our e-mails at the office that we miss the fluke of a whale as it breaches. Some months ago, in February of 2013, God gave me a gift.

I try to be "present"—to remain in the moment and prayerful so that I am aware of God's gifts. And on that special day in February, I received a gift of clarity. And my life has been different ever since. And it happened at an unlikely place for a miracle—at the gym. (Though I like to think if Jesus returned, he would be with us in our churches, and our markets and malls, in our coffee shops and fast food restaurants, and in our homeless shelters, in our homes and in our gyms—with us everywhere.)

I was riding an exercise cycle. I used to do BodyStep, but in one of my many "work-arounds," I reached a point when I couldn't do that any longer. So I adapted by biking. I had my own playlist on my iPhone, but I also had problems putting in my earbuds—it was requiring too finely coordinated motor skills.

The music was playing, but I dropped the earbuds. And in that moment, the world seemed to spin backwards for just a minute. All of a sudden everything went quiet, reduced just to my breaths. Those breaths accompanied by pure silence—the silence we all seek when we pray and want to achieve peace of mind. In that silence, I was incredibly self-aware that something was happening to me.

I looked around the gym—though it was almost like an out-of-body floating. Over by the bike where I was, there was a track. People were walking around the track. I looked into one face and then another, and in each countenance I gazed at, I could see how they were broken. I can't say how I knew, but I viewed it that my ALS was breaking through every one of my walls—those defenses I generally put up, even when I don't realize it or intend to.

I was frozen—just for a moment—then I scanned the next person, then the next. It was amazing! It was like a moment in a movie when the cinematographer pans across the whole crowd.

In some cases, I could see the brokenness. I could see it etched on their faces, or in the pain in their eyes. But everyone was suffering—whether I saw it or not—and I could feel all of it in my own body. We were all one person, all broken, all suffering.

The whole strange sensation lasted probably a good long minute or two. Even though I felt pain, I know God was also strengthening me, because I definitely felt equally a measure of peace and calm. I was certain that this was how Christ felt to walk among all the suffering. I was certain his acute awareness was so tuned in to people that he could indeed say to someone, "Rise and walk." He knew, placing his hands on a broken body, where that body—or soul—needed to be healed.

After this incident, I also felt this same sensation when handing out communion. As I looked in each supplicant's eyes, I tried to be fully present in my suffering and their suffering—creating an open flow of compassion.

So what did this mean for me? We walk around all put together, but we're actually all broken. We're falling apart. Think about it. Even in your own lives. What does broken mean to you?

We all walk around acting like everything is peaceful, happy. Perhaps this is nowhere more obvious than in a church. Occasionally, especially in a healthy church where people feel they can be fully authentic, you may find someone attending and revealing their grief. But often, we arrive in our Sunday best, with our Sunday best smiles. But Jesus sees what's beneath the Sunday best, what lies behind the smile.

In reality, some of us have physical pains that we see. But plenty more of us have emotional and spiritual pain. None of us have a life that is without any form of pain.

The addict. The loved ones of the addict.

Those in chronic pain. The caretakers of those in chronic pain.

The abused. The abusers.

There is a brokenness for every kind of wholeness.

I am grateful for glimpsing the brokenness.

I think of perhaps the most broken moment in the Bible. There are many to choose from. But I think of when Jesus asks, in Luke 22:42, if the cup can be taken from him. We all think we want the cup taken from us. I want my ALS gone.

It is a cup I never asked for.

But in fact, our broken pieces give us glimpses into the lives of others.

If I had my magic wand, I would make ALS go away from all of us. But I would not take away the burden only from me. I would not trade this glimpse at the broken wings of the broken sparrows.

And I know that it is God's Word that provides the bandage. And when we are all reunited in heaven, it will not be a bandage—because even a bandage over a cut will still leave a scar—but instead wholeness. We will all be perfectly unbroken, in a joyful pureness that we cannot even begin to imagine. We will be broken no more.

CHAPTER EIGHT

Baby Sparrows

Sometimes when you pick up your child you can feel the map of your own bones beneath your hands, or smell the scent of your skin in the nape of his neck. This is the most extraordinary thing about motherhood— finding a piece of yourself separate and apart that all the same you could not live without.

JODI PICOULT, *PERFECT MATCH*[1]

Whenever I think of being pregnant, I remember fondly when I didn't know yet that I was pregnant. It was late May 1997, and I met my parents, my sister, and my niece

---

1. Jodi Picoult, *Perfect Match* (New York: Washington Square Press, 2003), 151.

at Disney World in Florida. The five of us enjoyed a few days together in the "happiest place on earth" (albeit an awfully expensive happy place) and during that time we toured Epcot.

While there, an odd thing kept happening. While in one of the on-site restaurants, we accidentally received an extra drink—six drinks instead of five. But then it happened again. And again. Once we even got an entirely extra *meal*. This kept happening almost every time we ordered food and drinks. We talked about how odd to get that extra soda so frequently—and at different restaurants around the property. It became a family inside joke—one that amused us, but anyone outside the family might just shrug.

About three weeks later, I walked into my client's facility, through the front doors, near the cafeteria. This was long before there was a nudge in my heart, pushing me toward seminary. I walked past the cafeteria and felt a ravenous hunger overtake me. I needed a bacon, egg, and cheese sandwich on whole wheat bread. I didn't want the bacon, egg, and cheese, I *needed* it, in a way only pregnant women can understand. I had to have it—and if it wasn't completely against my nature and impossible, I might even have pushed someone out of the way to get that sandwich—just cut in line and demanded my sandwich— now! Of course, I didn't do that. But I was craving something I never ate.

My intuition—my burgeoning mother's intuition (you know, that intuition that gives women superpowers, like eyes in the back of our heads to tell us when our kids are causing trouble in the backseat of the car)—told me something was going on inside of me. I went home that night and took a pregnancy test.

No little blue line.

So I threw away the test and went to walk the dogs. When I got home, something told me to look in the trash can.

There, nestled on the top of the trash, was my test. And now there was definitely a blue line.

And then I promptly felt like throwing up.

Once I figured out how to avoid feeling nauseated, with saltines and ginger ale, I loved being pregnant. I filled my bras better, felt like an uber-woman in charge of my changing body, and worked right up until I was in active labor. I didn't gain a lot of weight, maybe twenty-five pounds, and nursing made the pounds melt away. (Don't hate me.)

Christopher Matthew Durant made me a mom, and I had no clue how fiercely a mother could love. I thought I knew what love was. I loved my mother and my father. I loved my grandmother and my sister. And I was madly in love with Matt. But this was different. I would have sawed off my arm, without anesthesia, if I thought Christopher's life would be better for the sacrifice. When he started day care, I felt like my heart was outside my body. The first day he was there, I ached all day, as if I had physically lost a limb and had phantom pain. But he liked day care and thrived, and the caregiver, Tammy, adored him, which made my decision easier—but only slightly.

Motherhood was everything I had hoped for and more.

The second time around, the pregnancy surprised me, and I was no less delighted. Before I had become pregnant, I had fervently prayed for a blue-eyed, blonde baby girl, with banana curls, but when my period was late, multiple pregnancy tests came back negative. Certain I had an ovarian cyst, I went to the doctor, and a blood test told the truth better than the home tests.

Once again, I faced nausea throughout growing my baby girl, but I now tell her she was custom-ordered. She is blonde, with blue eyes, and had banana curls for a while.

My water broke around two o'clock in the morning, soaking the bed. I remember being insulted when Matt responded to the announcement by saying he would get a dog towel to clean up. We had time for breakfast at the hospital, hours later, and I cried, because I didn't think I could love another baby as much as I loved my first. Since then, I've learned this is a common fear among women. And it's unfounded. When that pink bundle was placed in my arms, I was rapturously, totally, completely in love.

Kathryn Gail Durant looked exactly like her brother at first glance, but she quickly changed. Because we were the only second-time parents with a newborn that day, the hospital asked to use her to demonstrate giving a baby a bath. She was the perfect model for the demonstration. Just as she is my perfect young woman today.

I would never, of course, put the onus of perfection on my children. It's a different kind of perfect. There is the "perfect" idea of the perfect straight-A student, with perfect attendance, and perfect manners, and perfect attitude, who always remembers to say "please" and "thank you," and is never disobedient. I don't know where they store those children, but I didn't get that model. Instead, I got the different kind of perfect, the godly kind of perfect. I got the perfect children for me, so matched that I feel as if my heart is a puzzle with four pieces, and when I, Matt, and our son and daughter put our pieces together, the puzzle fits. My children are perfect because they breathe. They live. They are loved.

This is also not to say I am one of "those" mothers who believe their children can do no wrong. As I said, I don't know where they store those models—and I wouldn't want one of those. I want my perfectly imperfect heart's treasures. My children. Just as any mother reading this wants only her child.

Motherhood, I have found, is both joyful and terrifying. While as babies, they were adorable and smelled like heaven with soft skin and cooing little gurgles, as they grew, we had fun—and not fun. The older our children get, the more I know their boo-boos can no longer be fixed with a chocolate cookie and Mommy's kiss followed by a SpongeBob bandage. Their hurts and ups and downs are more complicated now—let alone that they have been burdened by a mother who is ill.

I've always been amazed that we created them and I incubated them. I enjoy them as teenagers now, and I see much of what we've taught them, the values, played out as they negotiate the world. It's incredibly hard to give them increasingly more responsibility, because I still feel like my heart is walking around outside my body. I can't stand that they're hurting because I'm afflicted with a terminal illness. Thankfully, my disease isn't genetic.

ALS makes mothering really difficult. I can't bake cookies anymore, or have a real-time conversation. The kids go to their father by default. He's the one who can go anywhere with them and do anything. It doesn't help that I'm the more serious parent, and was even before I was diagnosed. I was always the "let's sit down and have a talk about this" parent, and Matt the "fun" one.

Since my diagnosis, what was once fluid is less so. In most marriages, we assume roles. We don't realize we do this—and so once again the hidden "blessing" of ALS made us cognizant of this. We assume roles and identities that maybe we had not intended. ALS has given us all an opportunity to examine that.

They all have to try to include me, when asking permission, informing of plans, and generally just sharing information. Mostly, each day, I am so grateful that I'm the one who's sick, and it's not one of them.

However, I know one day I will leave them. The natural order of things is parents die first. When this doesn't occur, and a child dies, the pain for the parents is overwhelming—many marriages don't survive. I am grateful the natural order will not be upended by my death. But I know that my passing will be too early. And that is unfair in the way that . . . well, life is unfair.

Perhaps I am most "angry" (and yes, even though I am a priest, and a Christian, I get angry) that ALS has taken the next step or stage from us.

We have stages of parenting. There is pregnancy, eating for two, and caring for our bodies as a home for the new baby. There is infancy, when the baby relies on Mama for everything, even the very life-giving milk that flows from her breast. Following this is the "terrible twos" when independence is asserted. And so it goes, with each progressive stage taking a child to manhood or womanhood.

It is usually adolescence that is the most fraught. They are learning to balance the teachings of Matt and me with their evolving personhood and their own choices. This is when teens rebel. And in a sense, this is when they should. This is when they are figuring it all out, or trying to. As a priest, I have counseled so many families; I can say without a doubt that most parents know their teens are going to make mistakes along the way. They just hope it is a mistake that isn't life-altering or worse, life-threatening. Drinking and driving, an unplanned teen pregnancy, an episode of horrible bullying, dropping out of school, whatever it is you pray—and believe me when I say the knees of countless parents have hit the floor praying for their teens—that they come through relatively unscathed.

What waits on the other side is friendship. The "policing" stage of adolescence ends, and the child is a grown man or woman. Hopefully, in healthy relationships, what happens next is a new closeness, a different kind of closeness. You become a "rabbi"—from Jesus's day: a teacher, a "counselor," if you will. They will hopefully come to you for advice, and then go off and consider that advice before making a decision. They come to discover you really *do* know something.

> Her children rise up and call her happy;
> her husband too, and he praises her . . .
> PROVERBS 31:28

I am not going to get to be that person for my children. That has been stolen from me, and that role will be for Matt and Matt alone.

Alone.

And that is hardly fair. Not fair for him. Or my son. Or my daughter. Or me.

But I know this.

I raised my baby sparrows in a nest of God's love. Jesus, God, and the Holy Spirit were a part of our daily lives. We invoked their names during grace and at bedtime prayers. We taught our children to love others as they love themselves. And so the next step was going to be to send the baby sparrows, our fledglings, from the nest and see if they could fly.

Of this I am confident: Raised with Christ in their lives, they are ready to soar. Christ is the air beneath their wings. He will sustain them when I can no longer.

And so my sparrow-darlings, though I can no longer speak, I can pray. And pray I do, for both of you every day, and for all the baby sparrows in our universe, negotiating a fast-moving world where the rules, in some ways, are constantly changing.

Hopefully, they know, our nest is always open.

CHAPTER NINE

Forgiveness and Redemption

Now there is a final reason I think that Jesus says, "Love your enemies." It is this: that love has within it a redemptive power. And there is a power there that eventually transforms individuals.

MARTIN LUTHER KING, JR.[1]

We do not forgive the way God does.

Jesus was perfect. God is perfect. The Holy Spirit is perfect. We are not.

---

1. *The Papers of Martin Luther King, Jr: Symbol of the Movement—January 1957-December 1958* (Oakland, CA: University of California Press, 2000), 321.

So it makes sense, then, that God forgives perfectly, and we do not. I know this firsthand because, oddly, through the "gift" of ALS, I have learned more about forgiveness and redemption than I ever learned when I was able-bodied.

For example, believe it or not, priests are imperfect people. My wonderful husband and I fight just like other couples fight. He does things that irritate me. I do things that irritate him (but, of course, *his* irritating things are worse than mine; oh, who am I kidding?).

ALS has taught me about forgiveness in ways I could never have imagined.

One of Matt's and my biggest fights since I was diagnosed was about, of all things, the handicapped van he bought. The van allows me to be wheeled over to the side of the vehicle and be "loaded in" like so much cargo. Like all of the other ways in which ALS has demanded I compromise, give up certain dignities, and accept losses, this was a "big deal" to me. However, Matt, like many men, was trying to be the family's provider and caretaker. He was handling it, efficiently, and without bothering me about it—at least that's how he viewed it. But to me, he was making a big purchase that represented loss. And I had, at that time, just about enough of loss.

So we had an argument. A big one. Except ALS even took *that* away from me. I considered this a serious argument. Matt defended his position. His response did nothing to convince me this purchase—made without consulting me—was the right choice. To reply, I had to move and bob my head, painstakingly utilizing the silver dot on my forehead to spell out my response, letter, by letter, by agonizing letter. Then my partner responded with another point he wanted to make.

And at that point, I gave up. I had a great point to make, but I realized explaining it all would take forever, letter by letter. So I thought *forget it*. Just too frustrating.

On the surface of things, in *this* world, I essentially "lost" my argument. However, on a deeper spiritual level, there was a powerful lesson. This big fight with Matt taught me so much about forgiveness, courtesy of this horrid disease. I needed to look at it from a perspective of Jesus Christ and the power of forgiveness and love.

> *The LORD is merciful and gracious,*
> *slow to anger and abounding in steadfast love.*
> *He will not always accuse,*
> *nor will he keep his anger forever.*
> *He does not deal with us according to our sins,*
> *nor repay us according to our iniquities.*
> *For as the heavens are high above the earth,*
> *so great is his steadfast love toward those*
> *who fear him;*
> *as far as the east is from the west,*
> *so far does he remove our transgressions*
> *from us.*
> PSALM 103:8–12

Humans get so upset at worldly issues. I am not about to say that humans should never fight or argue. Quite frankly, there are many, many issues that demand a response. I could go on and on, but at the bare minimum, obviously, we should confront loved ones about addiction issues, betrayals of trust, important matters related to children, and so on. However, what our van argument taught me was most of the time, if we silenced our tongue, the issue wasn't one worth yelling about or worth the discord.

However, we should not silence our tongue with resentments. We should silence our tongue with forgiveness.

Following Christ's example, we should act at all times with love and compassion. I know many people recall the time in the Bible when Jesus *did* lose his cool—when he overturned the moneychangers' tables in his Father's house. He had a strong point to make—and he rightfully wanted them out of his Father's house. But consider this: At the Last Supper, even as he knew his betrayer was sharing the meal with him, he still shared his Body and Blood.

Think of it. *Knowing* he was going to be sent to a painful, horrifying death, and terrible humiliation beforehand, he gave us the greatest gift: himself. *He gave us his Body and Blood to help ease the state of alienation between humankind and God.* (I italicized this because it's important, and I will remind us of this before the end of the chapter.) Every time we share Jesus himself—and in the Episcopal Church he is fully present in the wine and bread—we grow closer to him and closer to God, the Creator.

And he offered us this gift even as he knew he was to be delivered unto death.

And we humans argue about a van.

The incident with the argument about the van, though, went deeper, into forgiveness. If ALS taught me to hold my tongue and be more willing to let go of arguments that have little to do with eternity, with the importance of Christ, then it has also taught me to forgive.

I have two choices when I choose not to continue an argument with Matt. One, I can choose to not type letter by letter, because it truly isn't worth the effort—and I consider, again, what are the truly important arguments. However, I can still be angry inside. Or, far more in line with Christ's example, I can forgive.

However, when we forgive, we should forgive the way God forgives us.

God doesn't forgive us—only to remind us two days later that we failed. God forgives us totally. We are pure again in his sight.

Think about that. Because that kind of forgiveness heals. It also brings us to the topic of redemption.

Christ's way promises *so* much more to us in both this life and the next.

> "... *Come to me, all you that are weary and are carrying heavy burdens, and I will give you rest. Take my yoke upon you, and learn from me; for I am gentle and humble in heart,*

and you will find rest for your souls. For my
yoke is easy, and my burden is light."

Matthew 11:28–30

These words in the Gospel of Matthew are Jesus's words. They are really the words of redemption.

I have a very serious question for you as you read this book: Aren't you tired?

Yes. Aren't you tired of carrying around your burdens and resentments? Are you weary of your grudges? I know I am.

So many of us carry resentments and burdens around like heavy weights. When we go to church or Bible study, or when we have moments with loving friends, we put down our burdens for a moment. We feel so light! This is the glory of redemption in Jesus Christ. We are free! Can you not feel how light your heart is?

But what do we do? No sooner do we set down our burden, than we take it up again.

We put on the yokes of shame, grudges, and anger. And they are heavy, heavy yokes indeed. They are not godly yokes. They are not the yokes of Jesus Christ.

How do I know? Read Jesus's promises. He is *gentle*.

His yoke is light.

He forgives you.

For a moment, I would like you to think about what you carry. How heavy is that burden? Pray and confess this burden to God. Pray earnestly and from the heart. If it helps, imagine I am next to you, holding your hand. We are filled with the Spirit.

God forgives you. As a priest, I know this to be so. We are *redeemed* through Christ. I wrote earlier of redemption. In the Body and Blood of Christ, he offers redemption. He eases the state of alienation between God and us. Without Jesus, without his promises in the Gospels, our lives would be emptier.

When Jesus forgives and redeems us, he spreads wide his arms. You can see, like Thomas did, the holes in his wrists, in the space of Destot—that spot in the wrists that supported him as he was nailed to the Cross. Think of his sacrifice for you. And finally, if he *died* for you, in that agony, on that Cross, isn't it time you said "thank you" for the redemption he offers, to walk the way he walked, to forgive the way he forgives?

There are no "take-backs" like in playground games. When God forgives, he forgives for keeps. When he redeems, he is saying, "Come all who are weary."

And now it is time for you to accept that gift.

And now is the time to offer that gift of *pure* forgiveness and redemption to others.

If Christ can sit with Judas at the Passover table, we all can sit with our "difficult" relatives at the Thanksgiving table.

CHAPTER TEN

The Oak Tree

*If childlike dependence on God is the mark
of a great soul, then there are great souls
hidden in in places where the world sees only
disability, decay, and despair.*

COLLEEN CARROLL CAMPBELL[1]

A giant oak tree overlooks Lucia House, littering the deck
with acorns, like children's LEGOs on a rug.

I roll down the ramp, and the oak seems to pitch more
acorns at my head, but they bounce off me and crunch
under my wheels. Making the second turn, I see the oak

---

1. Colleen Carroll Campbell. *My Sisters the Saints: A Spiritual Memoir*
(New York: Crown Publishing Group, 2012), 52.

tree's strong trunk, mottled brown, like the inside of a Snickers bar, and I know from previous experience, the darkest brown faces not the elements, but lies against the tree's center. Far from uniform, the trunk and its bark have bumps and knots, scrapes, and even burrowed-out sections, where creatures have nested. The tree's been standing for years, probably hundreds, a strong tower and testimony to life.

I think of us—human beings. How many people are like me? From the outside, I no longer am the strong and graceful ballerina. I appear weak and disabled. What about those we look at, weathered by illness, addiction, depression? So many of us have burrowed-out places where we have sustained great injury to our bodies—and our hearts. I think of the grief-stricken, bowed by the pain they feel.

I think of these things from time to time, but then I roll on past and into my week. I see the tree every time I come and go from my office. But the past six days, in the depths of my own heartache, I really noticed. It's not been an easy week. The list bearing the names of people who especially need prayer keeps growing. These are people I love, and people I may not know but who are instead prayed for and loved by those in my beloved flock.

The prayer list is a daily and weekly reminder that people we love are physically sick, visually declining, psychologically depressed, spiritually bereft. Some have died;

we all will. September 11 doesn't pass anymore without remembering significant loss. As a nation, we were joined on that day, and the days that followed. In Yankee Stadium, following that horrible day our nation endured, there was a prayer event attended by the faithful of multiple Protestant denominations, along with Catholics, Muslims, Sikhs, and Hindus (and probably others as well). Yet as the years have passed, we have drifted from each other again. Like the battered oak, we have weathered so much together—and separately.

I look at the oak, admiring my Creator who gifted this earth with such magnificent beauty as this tree. I need that reassurance of God's hand. This long and difficult week began with an abrupt reminder that life's utterly unpredictable, and we're vulnerable: just before nine in the morning, Albemarle High School implemented "lockdown," telling everyone something or someone threatened the safety of the people inside the campus. Now I have to confess, I'm the mother of two teenagers who love country music, and I could just hear my son, who attends Albemarle High, singing Billy Currington's song "People Are Crazy."

But as the morning slipped by, the song ceased being funny, and everyone inside evacuated to nearby schools. Rumors raged, by text and Twitter. An intruder had been detained, and while ultimately nothing bad happened, students, teachers, staff, and parents recalled

Virginia Tech, Sandy Hook, and Columbine. How have we become a nation where "lockdown" exists in our schools? But then I recall some older congregants discussing the "nuclear" drills in schools during the Cold War. Children were told to climb under their desks, and brace for a nuclear bomb—as if a wooden desk could save schoolchildren and their teachers from a Hiroshima-like event.

Can we really be protected from bad things? The truth is awful things happen, including to people we love, and our helplessness adds pointed pain to the constant ache of sadness and regret. But the tree over at Lucia House is constant, too. The great oak bends in the wind, and drinks the rain, nourished by every storm. It remains long after some of us will pass.

Then, midweek, I received a text message from a friend. "This living and loving thing," she wrote, "It's risky." Oh, but it is. And I know she's right. She knows, perhaps better than some, that loving leaves us vulnerable to significant pain, as well to unbounded joy. You don't need to have lost someone close to you to understand. Anyone who's ever had a pet knows we love the velvet off their ears, and their eyes seem to reveal everything they can't say. They walk with us, wonderful company, until one day, life leaves and the creature we adored is gone. Living and loving is terribly risky.

I know my friends, family, and congregants will miss me when I am gone. How could they not miss my wonderful self! Loving me is risky. But then again, none of us knows precisely what the future will bring. Yes, living and loving is risky. And the fact is that the scariest things, the most awful things, will be those we cannot imagine because our mind doesn't dare let us think such thoughts: 9/11, ALS, a gunman on a campus. They are beyond the unseen boogeyman beneath our bed.

But I know this, when we love and then experience loss, and when we're hurting, the likelihood we'll need forgiveness or to forgive increases. Just as a threatened animal bites, stings, or sprays, our fight-or-flight instinct explodes into action. Our limbs or tongues lash out, pain masquerading as anger, and we strike, as though delivering a blow will provide an escape route for our angst. The target might be ourselves, if we think we could have done something different to prevent the pain, or disease. More often, we blame someone else: the doctor didn't do everything she could, or the other driver made a poor judgment call. Occasionally, there's no discernible scapegoat, save for the universe, or God Almighty: bad things happen. And like tit for tat, our agony from living and loving needs assuaging. Consciously or subconsciously, we want others to hurt because we do.

I know a woman so pained by the horrible actions of her church that she lifted the "bird" to the sky—because loving God and her church had been risky. Except she is mistaken. Loving a church is sometimes risky; loving God never is.

Just as the oak tree is good news for squirrels gathering acorns to savor this winter, the words from Scripture provide us with sustenance over the winter of our pain. God is always with us, standing before the danger to guide us; and God is there to provide a balm to our hearts when the bad things happen. This world is fallen. Bad things do happen because God's way and our way are likely very different, but we won't be abandoned. Our branches, like the oak's limbs, may be gnarled and knotted, but still we grow heavenward, closer to God.

The oaks standing for hundreds of years, from a time when this land was just forest, are a testament to a loving God. But when we are hurt, many of us tend to react with anger—whether that is toward God or those who hurt us.

But our faith must not be shaken. We must look to our roots, firmly planted in the soil of Christ. And we must keep our hearts open; we cannot let the fear of hurt or pain cause us to become cynics. The world has enough cynics. As Christians, we are called to abandon cynicism for hope.

I am reminded of Matthew 18:1-3 in which the disciples asked the Christ, "Who is the greatest in the kingdom of heaven?" Jesus replied, "Those who become like children."

In the book *Imagine: How Creativity Works* by Jonah Lehrer, there is a marvelous anecdote about Yo-Yo Ma. One of the most famous cellists in our day, he says, "When people ask me how they should approach performance, I always tell them that the professional musician should aspire to the state of the beginner. In order to become a professional," he says, "you need to go through years of training. You get criticized by all your teachers, and you worry about all the critics. You are constantly being judged. But if you get onstage and all you think about is what the critics are going to say; if all you are doing is worrying, then you will play terribly. You will be tight, and it will be a bad concert. Instead," Ma says, "one needs to constantly remind oneself to play with the abandon of the child who is just learning the cello."[2]

We're broken people, scruffier than the oak tree's bent branches and crumbling bark. We're painfully wounded by loving, living, and a whole lot of critiquing. Is it possible for us, despite the pain of this world, to love God with childlike abandon?

Perhaps we should think of the oak as a sign of God's promise. The oaks of Mamre were where Abraham sat, and where he constructed an altar. In Genesis 13, these oaks are where Abraham receives God's promises.

---

2. Jonah Lehrer, *Imagine: How Creativity Works* (New York: Houghton Mifflin Harcourt, 2012), 110–111.

I look at the oak tree again. This time, I smile. Yes, those acorns are a pain in the neck when I am rolling over them in my chair, but I know God's promises. You see, this chair is my burrowed-out place. It's a place of deep pain for me, for my family, and those who love me. But one day, with every fiber of my broken body, I know—I know right down to my DNA and my carbon atoms—that God has promised I will dance in heaven. And so even in this week—this week when I am reminded that we are a broken people in a broken world—the oak reminds me to be childlike. To instead see the oak's branches the way a child would, as a place to climb, as shelter from the sun, as a tree growing toward heaven.

As a promise.

CHAPTER ELEVEN

Sparrow of Peace

Give yourself peace of mind.

HANNAH ARENDT

I have told Matt, and my closest friends, and my wonderful "boss" here at my beloved church, that when I can no longer participate in the Lord's Supper, fully being present with the flock at this sacred meal, then it will be time for me to leave.

I love so much about being a priest. I love everything about it. Even the worst days in my priesthood surpass my career before this one. But the Lord's Supper? That is grace to me.

But to fully understand why I love it, I need to talk about peace. You see, my readers, if you've journeyed this whole way with me, you will remember when I first got my diagnosis. I wept.

However, "weeping" to me is that sort of lofty-sounding "Hollywood cry." Ever notice how in a romantic comedy, if there is a scene when the heroine cries, she still looks fantastic? That's weeping. What I did upon learning my diagnosis was a "messy sob." You know the kind. Tissues balled up all over the place, puffy face, eyes swollen shut, unable to complete a sentence because you're gasping. I am not an "attractive crier."

But here I am, nearing the end of my time on earth. And I am at peace.

You see, none of us know when we are going to go. I might be wheeled into oncoming traffic by accident tomorrow! What a spectacularly bizarre and ironic turn of events that would be. However, I know my time is probably closer than yours. And I know *what* will kill me. I may not know when—but I know what. My nemesis.

Yet I have made my peace because I know I am going to heaven, and there I will meet the ultimate healer. I will sup with him; I will be healed, shedding this earthly body to dance on the clouds.

That's what the Lord's Supper promises. That's why when I am in Jesus Christ's *presence,* his real and actual presence in the wine and bread, I am overjoyed, moved with emotion, rapturous. I need to be fed at that table.

Peace I leave with you; my peace I give to you.

JOHN 14:27A

Now, I'd like to talk for a moment about sandwiches. When the rock musician Warren Zevon was dying of terminal illness, one of his greatest fans, the usually subversive David Letterman, devoted an entire show to Zevon.[1] No laughter. A real and deep discussion. Zevon's death was imminent.

At one point, toward the end of the interview, David Letterman addresses the elephant in the room: Death. You see, as we have moved away from small towns and farming cultures, when we witnessed the life and death of animals, or the death of a loved one laid out at home in the parlor, it has become something we are extremely uncomfortable with. For a talk show host, Letterman was brave.

He asked Warren Zevon a question. In light of the fact, Letterman said, that Zevon, barring the proverbial bus hitting Letterman as he crossed the street, was closer to that veil between life and death, what did *he* know that Letterman did not? What advice did he have to share?

---

1. http://ultimateclassicrock.com/warren-zevon-on-david-letterman/ (Accessed July 22, 2015)

Zevon's reply? He wished he had eaten more sand-wiches. This was his metaphor for being in the moment, for saying "yes," for enjoying life.

From the outside, Zevon certainly was at peace. I admired his calm even though I did not yet know I would walk a path of terminal illness.

As a priest, I know this. The peace of Jesus promised in the Lord's Supper "passeth all understanding."[2] I truly believe—and will preach this to my dying day, whenever that is—that we all have a God-shaped hole in our hearts and souls. A hole only Jesus can fill. And we don't know *real* peace until we acknowledge and accept that. Despite the promises of this world, despite the promises of peace that some think comes from a bottle, or a pill . . . or even a sandwich . . . peace can only come from our Lord.

As a person with ALS, as a *Christian* with ALS— forgetting my collar for the moment—I know that I could not be at this moment in my life without Jesus. I could not be unable to speak, increasingly and terrifyingly less able to swallow, unable to move, unable to laugh, unable to so much as scratch an itch, unable to hug the ones I

---

2. One of the blessings a priest can give at the end of the Eucharist: "The peace of God, which passeth all understanding, keep your hearts and minds in the knowledge and love of God, and of his Son Jesus Christ our Lord; and the blessing of God Almighty, the Father, and the Son, and the Holy Ghost, be amongst you, and remain with you always. Amen." The Book of Common Prayer (1979), 339.

love, and feel this certain of where I will wake up after death, a place so glorious it is beyond our human imaginings, without God. I could not look at my children, husband, and mother, knowing I will leave them sooner than I wish, and be able to accept that, hopefully courageously, without the Holy Spirit.

I need the Father, the Son, and the Holy Spirit.

And I need, I deeply need, the Lord's Supper.

For it is then I keenly feel what Jesus promised in the Gospel of John. He leaves me Peace. His Peace. The God-shaped Peace. The Peace of God which passeth all understanding.

Think of Jesus in that moment. Locked in the Upper Room with his closest friends. He predicts his death. He predicts his betrayal by one sitting with him and eating. He predicts that Peter—the one he loved most—would deny him three times in the most painful abandonment of his journey to the cross.

Yet, he breaks bread. He blesses it. He shares it. Then he shares something far more precious: himself. He promises that when we sup in remembrance of him, in this sacred meal, we will be given his grace and peace.

Jesus's legacy was never riches. Some denied him because they expected a Savior, a Messiah, with a literal army. One that would cast out the corruption of Rome. But Jesus's legacy was instead one of a man who dined with sinners, who healed the untouchable, who performed miracles, who enjoyed a wedding with his friends. His was a legacy of the Prince of Peace.

His symbol, of course, one of many for our Lord, is a dove. But today, as I write this book and I near the end, I like to think he is a fellow sparrow. The Sparrow of Peace.

CHAPTER TWELVE

A Sparrow Flies

All that we love deeply becomes part of us.

HELEN KELLER

I have stepped down from my position in my church. This decision was not made lightly, and was made with the advice of my spiritual advisers, consulting with my husband. But I am no longer able to participate in the sacred meal I described in the last chapter. And I already miss that sustenance.

So now it is time to say good-bye. But I believe, fully, that this is not the end. It is instead my new, whole beginning, shedding this earthly body that no longer serves me well. It was a vessel for my soul, and it is time for me to fly.

I read a book once about explaining death to children by Dr. Sally Downham Miller. She would use an egg. The example she used was a little child who lost a parent. She had the child crack the egg. Then she asked her what she could use the "good stuff" for. The egg yolk and whites. They could be scrambled to give sustenance. They could be used in a cake or some other recipe on its way to becoming something else.

But once you crack and use the goodness inside, what is left?

Even a small child can see it is just "shells." A shell. Fragile. Broken. No longer of use to the inside of the egg. There's no putting the egg back. No, the egg is better off in its new life. It no longer needs that shell.

Just as I no longer need mine.

But I don't want to leave without summarizing what this book was all about. Because I hope as you arrive at this chapter with me, that you have gulped the air of Israel, walked the path I once did when I was able-bodied, that path of Jesus. I hope you realize that even in the face of darkness, of illness, of terminal illness, of disability, of loss, and even of death, that grace and miracles abound.

Even in my saddest moments, I knew God was with me. And every time I felt a little bit tenuous about that, a little unsure—just a little—God would grant me some miracle of my own. Whether it was seeing suffering in the gym, or the miracles of motherhood in my own life, whether the miracle of Jesus's presence in coincidences—or in the very intentional meal at the altar—I was always certain of God's call.

You see, God knows every sparrow. Even though they could be bought centuries ago for pennies, the Bible tells us they do not fall without God knowing. God knows the lilies of the field, clothed in white purity. So I am certain, with a certainty I feel in every cell in my body, that God knows you by name. God named you and claimed you, for our Creator loves you that much.

God knows my name too.

So despite what I face, I know that the Lord is saying, "Jennifer, my good and faithful servant, you may come to me for rest. Come to me for peace. Jennifer, you may fly home. I am waiting with open arms."

And so, one day, shall our Savior call for you too.

With God, Jesus Christ, and the Holy Spirit, we are always home.

Epilogue

Jennifer Durant lost her courageous battle with ALS shortly after completing the chapters of this manuscript, on Ash Wednesday, February 18, 2015.

Jennifer labored over this manuscript, painstakingly working, typing letter by letter with the aid of her assistive devices. She had lengthy discussions before ALS took her voice, and via typed communications, with her family, friends, and editor, was unable to truly rest until she knew the book was done.

She wrote *Sparrow* with incredibly humble intentions. This was never, ever about "her" or the "ego" of being published. She wrote this book to bring Christians more fully to Christ—and to hopefully reach those who have yet to accept Jesus as their Savior. Written even to those who have drifted from God because of painful circumstances in their lives, unhealthy churching, untenable loss, or those who felt they were not "lovable;" those who could not see the beauty Jennifer saw in people from every walk of life, sinners and saints alike.

Even when Jennifer could no longer speak, she never stopped trying to spread God's message. And she somehow "shined," radiating a positive glow to all around her, so sure was she in Jesus's love. Before we make her sound like a saint, she would be the first to playfully drop an "oh fudge" or some other modified colorful expression, the first to tell you that though she had readers when the ALS took her speaking ability, she always had to deliver the, as she called it, "punch line" during a sermon. She would be the first to tell you how utterly human she was—just like all of us.

Jennifer would hope that her story has brought you closer to God, and perhaps will be used in small group studies. Through these pages the remarkable Reverend Jennifer lives on in spirit, just as she lives on in heaven.

You may learn more about her and her life at: http:// jenniferdurant.com

Matthew P. Durant

Here's What I Said

Jennifer's Final Sermon

Church of Our Saviour, Charlottesville, Virginia
February 8, 2015
Isaiah 40:21–31
Mark 1:29–39

The gospel today is filled with Jesus curing people from sickness and from demons. There's Simon's mother-in-law, whose hand he takes, bringing her from life-threatening fever to serving her community. As the entire city arrives at the door, Jesus cures some and removes demons from others. The text is clear. He cured many. Jesus didn't cure them all. Then, like a shadow disappearing into inky darkness, he disappeared to pray.

While the text doesn't reveal the conversation, I have some ideas. Cutting his baby teeth on Isaiah's words:

Have you not known? Have you not heard?
Has it not been told you from the beginning?
Have you not understood from the foundations
  of the earth?
It is he who sits above the circle of the earth.
ISAIAH 40:21–22A

I bet he poured out his soul for his beloved sick that
he couldn't cure and for the people's agony. I imagine he
lamented the unfairness to those who face devastating
diseases and demonic possession. I see him even ques-
tioning the whole plan. At least the parts he knew about.
No doubt he sought wise counsel and strength for what
lay ahead. He needed endurance and undying faith that
no matter what he encountered, grace and love would
conquer the darkness.

Jesus, the perfectly human deity, must have felt concern for Simon's mother-in-law, sick with fever. We know
he wept upon hearing about Lazarus's death. And we
know he exorcised dozens, even thousands, of demons.
No doubt he sought solitude to rage against injustice, to
beg for suffering's elimination, to somehow permanently
eliminate demons from the world. Yet the prophet Isaiah
would ground him.

Have you not known? Have you not heard?
The LORD is the everlasting
  God, the Creator of the ends of the earth.

He does not faint or grow weary;
    his understanding is unsearchable.
He gives power to the faint,
    and strengthens the powerless.

ISAIAH 40:28–29

Every 12-step program requires admitting you're powerless against your addiction. Well, while I had hoped to never speak the initials in a sermon again, I must admit I'm powerless against ALS. This despicable, damnable, destructive disease is becoming unpredictable. And although God gives me strength every day, the amount ebbs and flows. Recently, I've noticed a significant drop in my energy level, which corresponds with how well I can function physically.

So with a broken heart and strong faith, I relay that my serving you liturgically is going to change. I sometimes can't hold up my own head. David and I, along with the wardens, will decide what happens next. The Holy Spirit will also have her say. And I love you.

You may have heard me tell this story. Years ago I dreamt I was walking through the woods, holding hands with a man who emanated love. As I chatted, telling him about my inadequacies, the man began to laugh from deep within his being. Then, he looked at me, and said with great joy and delight, "Jennifer, just be who you are, because when you are, you are absolutely fabulous." That encounter with Jesus is what's carrying me through this incredibly painful time.

> But those who wait for the LORD shall renew
>   their strength,
>   they shall mount up with wings like
>   eagles,
> they shall run and not be weary,
>   they shall walk and not faint.
>
> ISAIAH 40:31

Bible Study Guide

Jennifer desired that her book include study of the biblical Scriptures that she chose to accompany her story. Reflecting on Scripture can be done individually or within a group. A variety of methods can be used, and reading or hearing the passage from a variety of biblical translations can offer up new insights. A study Bible that has footnotes or sidebars of explanation can enhance individual and group reading.

The Aural Method (often called African Bible Study) *Time frame:* ½–1 hour

Three important principles govern this method of experiencing Scripture:

1. Confidentiality is always strictly observed. Whatever is said in the group of a personal nature is not to be repeated outside the group. It is not even a topic for subsequent conversation with the individual involved. "What is said here, stays here."

2. Participants are free to "pass" at any time if they cannot think of a response or do not wish to share it.

3. When a person is speaking to the group, the group simply listens with no response. No one person is to discuss what someone else has said, though sometimes another person's response may trigger a similar thought.

Steps:

1. A person appointed reads the passage aloud slowly. Before reading, allow a minute or so of silence as the leader reminds people to listen for the word or phrase that catches their attention.

2. Participants take a minute to recall in silence the word or phrase that caught their attention.

3. Beginning with the leader, each person says the word or phrase with the group (no more than just a word or phrase).

4. Someone else reads the passage.

5. Participants think about: "Where does this passage touch my life today"? (3–5 minutes of silence)

6. Each person shares these: "For me, . . ."

7. Someone else reads the passage out loud again.

8. Participants think about: "From what I have heard and shared, what does God want me to do or be

this week? How does God invite me to change?"
(3–5 minutes)

9. Each person shares these: "For me, . . ." The leader
reminds the group that each person will pray for
the person on their left, naming what they share in
this step, so they will want to listen carefully and
remember any specifics the person names.

10. Invite each person to pray for the person on their
left, naming what was shared in Step 9, and to
pray that prayer daily until the group meets again.
(Or, a general form prayer, for example, "Christ,
may your blessing be with _____. Fill her/
him with your love and grace.")

11. Say the Lord's Prayer together.

For variety, the following questions may be used:

- After the first reading, "What does this reading say
to you about God?"
- After the second reading, "What does this reading
say to you about who you are?"
- After the third reading, "What do you hear God
asking you to do or be this week?"

What follows is a listing of each of the chapters of
Sparrow, with one or two pieces of Scripture to delve
into related to the chapter. You may use any method you
choose to follow, including the one above. There are three

questions per chapter for going deeper in your reflections, whether individually or in a small group.

Light a candle. Begin with prayer. Be comfortable in silence. Let the Spirit speak to you.

Introduction

Read Matthew 10:26–33

Jesus speaks words of comfort and reassurance. His message is not a secret, but intended to be shouted from the housetop (the traditional place from which public announcements were made). The disciples may do this without fear since God's own loving power stands with them. According to the Gospel of Matthew, followers of Christ are to proclaim their faith through their actions and attitudes.

- In what areas of your life would you like to experience Jesus's healing and restoration? Approach Jesus and ask for his help?
- Where are you in your faith journey?
- When have you needed someone to "carry you" because of difficulty—emotional, physical, or spiritual?

Chapter 1

Read Jeremiah 29:11–14
and Philippians 4:1–14

From Jerusalem, Jeremiah writes to the exiles that are far from home. While in prison, Paul writes the Christians in Philippi. Both share the importance of a relationship with God. Jeremiah tells them that they will be restored and will return to their homeland one day. Paul appreciates the concern the Philippians have expressed for him, but all he needs is God.

- When have your plans had an unexpected change? How did you respond?
- Have you ever had to share joyful news with another person? What did it feel like—before, during, and after?
- Have you ever had to share bad news? What were your feelings then?

Chapter 2

Read Matthew 26:36–46

Matthew portrays Jesus as profoundly human in this passage. Jesus retreats from the approaching ordeal (his arrest and crucifixion) and prays to be delivered from it. However, he seeks strength to do God's will.

- When have you felt alone, despite being with others? How did you feel? How did you cope?
- In your experience, when you are intensely troubled and feel abandoned, what strength and comfort come through prayer?
- What changes would you like to make in your prayer life?

Chapter 3

Read Romans 8:18–27
and I Corinthians 13:4–13

Paul's letters to both the Romans and the Corinthians speak of living as God's children, waiting for what will to come in the future when we are united with Christ in a new creation. While the future may be unclear, it will be complete when God is fully revealed and we are fully known. As we wait, we are encouraged to follow the way of love.

- What does hope mean to you?
- When have you had to depend on others? On God? What was the turning point when you realized you needed help?
- Have you ever lost your voice, physically or figuratively? How did you compensate and communicate?

Chapter 4

Read Ephesians 4:1–16

Paul offers practical advice for everyday living. Live in unity. Grow spiritually mature and serve others. Seek spiritual renewal. Put others first. All in order to participate in the love of Christ.

- What are ways you can replace bitterness and anger with kindness, mercy, and forgiveness?
- What wisdom have you learned in creating (and keeping) a relationship with another person?
- How have you spoken the truth in love?

Chapter 5

Read Matthew 4:18–25

Follow me. In those simple words Jesus called twelve men to leave their families and jobs behind and follow him on his travels throughout Judea. Along the way he preached, taught, and healed those he encountered. His invitation continues today.

- When have you visited a site to walk in another person's footsteps, to see and experience what they had done in that same location before you?
- When have you felt the need to be carried by another person, either physically or metaphorically?
- How does the past impact our present and future?

Chapter 6

Read John 10:14–18

Shepherd imagery is used of God and human rulers throughout Scripture. An ideal leader, a shepherd shows selfless love and compassion toward those under his or her care. The word "good" implies more than moral strength or virtuous leadership; for Jesus, it meant deep care in a relationship that would be boundless in life as well as death.

- How is being a parent, spouse, partner, or friend like being a shepherd?
- When have you behaved like a good shepherd to someone? When has someone been your good shepherd?
- What signs of Jesus's working in your own life most clearly reveal his love and calling?

Chapter 7

Read Psalm 34 and Luke 22:39–46

The psalmist recounts God's deliverance, interspersed with invitations for others to look to and experience God. Luke shares the account of Jesus in the Garden of Gethsemane with his disciples, yet very much alone, as he is about to be betrayed and handed over to the authorities and ultimately his death.

- When have you had an insight on life during a time when you were most vulnerable?
- What does broken mean to you?
- What sustains you in time of trouble?

Chapter 8

Read Proverbs 31:10–31

This acrostic poem is in praise of a capable wife. While this tale of a heroic woman may seem far-fetched for the twenty-first century, it offers the blessings of wisdom, wealth, justice, generosity to the poor, reputation, children, and, most precious of all, a good spouse and partner.

- Have you ever acted upon a premonition or intuition? Why or why not?
- What does it mean to you to be "perfect"? How is this similar (or different) than being godly?
- How can parenthood or friendship be an example of wisdom in the biblical sense?

Chapter 9

Read Psalm 103 and Matthew 11:25–30

God does whatever is needed to enhance life. Righteousness and justice are for all who follow God. For Matthew, the innocent and simple surpass the wise. Instead of a heavy burden of rules and regulations, we can hand everything over to Jesus and imitate his gentleness and humility.

- When have you been angry—*really* angry? For what reason and how did you deal with your anger?
- What can we learn from God (and Jesus) about anger? Forgiveness?
- When have you been forgiven? When have you forgiven someone?

Chapter 10

Read Matthew 18:1–19

To become like a child is to take a position of extreme vulnerability. Greatness in the kingdom will be for those who admit their smallness before God and have an attitude of childlike (not childish) trust. We should take care of those who may be immature or weak in faith. Temptations to stumble will always arise, but we must remain grounded in God.

- What is the "oak" in your life? What keeps you grounded?
- When have you allowed yourself to be vulnerable like a child?
- What would it take for you to love God with abandon?

Chapter 11

Read John 14:18–30

Chapter 14 of John's Gospel is characterized by a spirit of profound peace and comfort as Jesus prepares his disciples for his imminent death and for their work after his departure. His parting gift to his disciples is peace, not like the "Have a nice day" kind of peace that humans exchange, but real peace, soul-deep peace.

- Jesus understood that external circumstances are often the source of many fears. How would you define Jesus's peace?
- In what sense do we defeat evil through our obedience to Jesus?
- Consider the time that may be left to you before Jesus comes to take you to be with him. What greater works would you like to do in your remaining time?

Chapter 12

Read Matthew 6:25–33

Human needs and desires should be more than food and clothing. These radical ideas of Jesus are anxiety provoking. We can counter these feelings with trustful attitudes. God cares for all creation and places special value on human creatures. Life will always include problems, but one who trusts God will live in the present and not anticipate future trouble.

- In what ways does anxiety distract you from your true priorities?
- What treasure do you value most profoundly? How consistent is it with seeking first God's kingdom and God's righteousness?
- Which of your priorities need to be reordered?